"Rather than moral imperatives descended from an ancient mount, Dr.Bill's Ten Demandments are relationship imperatives distilled from his elevated perspective on modern organizational dynamics. Leaders will benefit from the content; exceptional leaders will equip their teams to excel, together."
Rev. Cameron Kirker, H.I.S. International

"I have been working to help CEOs and COOs and company presidents since 1993 and I can't think of a better introduction to team building than Dr.Bill has put together here."
Raymond Prill, President, ERO-Executive Resource Organization

"The Ten Demandments is an excellent resource to allow you to rethink traditional practices and create opportunities to unleash the often hidden value-added contributions of all employees."
Richard Rogers, V.P. Human Resources, Wayne Memorial Hospital

"This book is an essential reading for all executives. Dr.Bill has captured the elements of successful leadership in a quick and easy to read format. Following his Demandments will make us all better leaders."
Roy Santarella, Executive V.P. & CAO, West Penn Allegheny Health S

"The greatest value in this book is that it takes truisms and gives them voice. It is a reminder of the essential and timeless wisdom of the workplace."
John Sena, Ph.D., Professor, Ohio State University

"The Ten Demandments offers clear insights to improve organizational team performance. It provides key behaviors needed for teams to succeed which any leader will find beneficial."
John Solheim, President/CEO St.Peter's Hospital

Diana,
Enjoy
Bill

2010

Dr. Bill's Ten Demandments for Leaders:

Leadership Imperatives for Exceptional Teamwork and Outstanding Results

By

Dr. Bill Moskal

Dr. Bill's Ten Demandments for Leaders: Leadership Imperatives for Exceptional Teamwork and Outstanding Results

Copyright 2010 by Dr. Bill Moskal

All rights reserved. No part of this book may be used or reproduced in any manner whatsoever without written permission from Dr. Bill Moskal, except as provided by the United States of America copyright law or in the case of brief quotations embodied in articles and reviews. The scanning, uploading, and distribution of this book via the Internet or via any other means without the permission of the publisher is illegal and punishable by law.

Please purchase only authorized electronic editions and do not participate in or encourage electronic piracy of copyrighted materials. Your support of the author's rights is sincerely appreciated.

Printed in the United States of America.

First Printing: 2010

Dedication

- Gilda, my wife, best friend, and special spirit. It is no coincidence that we are together.

- Diane Evangelista-Moskal, my late wife (1946-2002), was most instrumental in helping me pursue my graduate work, and was the primary person and best friend who always wanted the best for me... her unconditional belief that I needed to ..."*be happy and spread your wings*"

- My mother, my dear "Mashka," for always believing that *"Billy is the best"* and for her unconditional love.

- My Dad for his kind, gentle, supportive, and caring ways in which he loved me.

- My son Christian and daughter-in-law Prital and my granddaughters, Shaysha and Aanvee, for their love and understanding and for keeping me grounded in reality.

- And of course, Basil and Izzi, our two Bichons Frise.

Dr. Bill's Ten Demandments for Leaders

Acknowledgements

- Gilda Hayes-Moskal, my wife, for her help in writing the manuscript, her patience, her questioning, her challenges (especially to my writing) and most importantly for her "supportive nudging" to keep it going!

- Ann McIndoo, my writing coach, for her guidance and insights and continuous and consistent "you can do it" and "great job" encouragements.

- Zenon Tomyn, of ZenOn Design, for his creative mind and belief in my work and for the beautiful cover artwork.

- My clients, both past, current, and future. I was most fortunate to work with leaders that truly believed in the human spirit.

Contents

Introduction 11

Demandment One: Team Cultures: If You Have Seen One Team, You Have Seen One Team 17

Demandment Two: Freedom Requires Structure 27

Demandment Three: Building the A.R.C. 41

Demandment Four: No Obstacles; Only Opportunities 51

Demandment Five: Awareness of Members' Value 63

Demandment Six: Ripple Effect; Reaction Outcomes 73

Demandment Seven: Recognize and Reward Teams First, Stars Second 81

Demandment Eight: Ownership is Everything 93

Demandment Nine: Trust, the Leadership Essential 107

Demandment Ten: It's About the People 119

Introduction

Early on I learned simple truths about leadership as a result of special parents who focused on my well being. My mother always reminded me that it was important to smile when meeting others; they feel noticed and they'll remember you. I learned a secondary benefit, too, that in so doing, I was also waiting to talk which made me a better listener. People trust that I hear them and this trusting facilitates dialogue. These simple guidelines have helped me to encourage leaders to acknowledge others and to listen with a "third ear" for information that may have gone unnoticed. Leaders should always be curious seekers of information on their path to goal attainment. Leaders must ask questions because the more we ask, the less likely we will tell.

My early mentor, Morrel Clute, shared his leadership insights with me one evening at a local café following one of his inspiring lectures. I asked him, "What does it take to move from managing to leading?" His response made a lasting impression on me. He said, "Managers tell others what to do, leaders ask questions." The paradigm shift is a move from Telling to Asking. Granted, there will be occasions when telling is necessary, but it has been my experience that leaders use it far too often.

I challenged a group of 20 hospital department Directors to take the next work day of 10-12 hours and to ask questions during every encounter with their team's members, both individually and collectively. I challenged them to keep a mental log of their dialogue with their subordinates and to track their success with asking questions. For example, if they were approached by an employee who had an issue to be resolved, the director's position was to ask questions, such as, "What is the source of the problem?" They must wait for a response and then ask a follow-up probing question. The directors were challenged to ask a minimum of three and up to five questions during the interaction. As expected, our follow-up meeting two days later produced more laughter and soul-searching than results.

As leaders managing projects and people, we are not promoted or hired because we ask questions. We are selected because we fit the profile that mimics the recruiter and the boss that chose us. We produce results and results require speed and answers – a process often fraught with peril -- but when leaders realize that team members do not produce when told or are forced into a corner, we see

Introduction

new leadership character blossoming with leaders pulling out all the stops. During crises, leadership is not developed; it is revealed.

After 30 years of facilitating team seminars, team retreats/advancements, and team coaching with senior leadership, I came to the conclusion that those leaders who listen, question, and observe are true Mentors. Those who take a different path of telling, pushing, and prodding are Tormentors. I have seen them both. After many fulfilling years working with leaders both as an internal coach and an external consultant/coach, I was driven to put in writing "stuff" that could prove helpful. I liken it to "re-charging one's battery" because there will be times when our "staying power" is lacking.

My vision was to write a book that could serve as a "hip-pocket guide" for new and current leaders. I knew from my experiences that leaders tend to give new models and ideas a cursory opportunity to succeed or survive. When new applications don't work, the tendency is to snap back to the status quo. Like the tension on a rubber band, as we pull away from our comfort zone, we tend to go back to a safe position. Not only do we have to learn new behaviors and ways of doing business, but we also have to recognize that the structures are much different with each circumstance. We are required, as leaders, to demand focused empathic behaviors of ourselves toward the people we have responsibility to lead and grow. We are required to demand of ourselves certain actions for the good of the people and the organization. Demanding of others is inappropriate. Demanding of ourselves is the key to our growth and development as leaders. As we demand of ourselves, we will provide the model that will engage others.

I was motivated by the realization after working with hundreds of teams that "if you've seen one team…you've seen one team." Teams are families encased in larger families, the organization. Each team has a unique way of interacting. They each have unique people and faces and skills and abilities. Each team is unique in the way they make decisions and the speed with which they communicate information to each other and to other teams.

Early in my professional career, I understood there was a better way to get to the end result that I wanted. It was clear to me that I would achieve more with others. I was also intrigued by the reaction that I received from others when I would introduce a different approach to solving a problem, or branding a product or service. Most were supportive; some were resistant or intimidated.

Introduction

I'm reminded of a teaching assignment that I had a faith-based high school. I was required to teach a world geography class for freshmen. The books had not arrived and it was now late September. Three weeks into the school year and I running out of motivational lectures on world countries. I did what I felt would work to engage the students and give them an experience "out side the box." I placed names of countries in a box and had each student draw a country. The country that they drew would become their obsession. I asked them to become the expert of the country. The second step was to "build a book". Each student was required to physically build their country with information and pictures. The goal was to have a complete book of world countries created by each of the students. Thirty eight countries in all. The process was a success. I was fired. Too much commotion and noise in the room that was disrupting the other classes was the rational. The structure was in place; however, the administration wasn't prepared for the abrupt change. I learned to give notice of my experiments and engage administration in the change process. Teach your boss!

Later in my education career, I was appointed Assistant Superintendent for Archdiocesan Schools in Detroit. I didn't have responsibility for operations, rather I was involved in the Peaceful Integration project. This was a parallel project to the Detroit Public Schools Desegregation project in the late 1970's. We were involved in the integration of numerous schools in the catholic districts. The integration effort involved three key and influential groups, students, parents, and the school personnel. As one would expect, the three affiliated groups were very different. They differed in their motivations, their suspicions, and of course their expectations. Each had to be structured to meet the expectations (purpose) and the requirements of the members. I had to work with each group separately before considering bringing the three groups together for a common purpose on common grounds. I learned that the structure, format and leadership were unique to each entity. Each entity had its own set of values. Each also was grounded in their own norms and mores. The values and the mores were not attacked, but rather supported and blended among the three entities. A beneficial component of the process was the collection of data. Similar questions were asked of each group and shared at the off-site events that were part of the change management process. The similarities in desires and purpose bonded the groups. Needless to say, the off-site events were froth with emotional obstacles that required a team of highly skilled facilitators to manage. The learning for me was the understanding that each team is unique and brings a set of unique skills to the table. Each team also has a very legitimate set of principles and a strong drive to succeed.

Introduction

As a consultant, my experiences were bountiful and filled with the joy of knowing that each team encounter would be different from the last tea development assignment. It was then, I coined the phrase, "If you've seen one team, you've seen one team." I consulted with healthcare teams as both an internal and external team facilitator and organization development specialist. Later in my career, I was fortunate to work with over fifteen Native American Tribal Clinics. The new learnings for me were a daily occurrence. From there it was to the Peace Corps in Ukraine facilitating cross-cultural teams in a newly independent country. The people in the Ukrainian business teams had expectations that were unrealistic by American standards. Helping them relate to real expectations with real outcomes and limited resources was a challenge for me and my MBA volunteers. I learned patience and humility and the power of engaging people by encouraging their skills. They had skills and abilities that rivaled our skills. The difference was they were not allowed to use their knowledge for their own personal; gain. It was truly a paradigm shift in thinking and behavior. I learned to enable people to open up and feel free to express themselves and take moderate risks.

In all of my experiences I was in a learning mode. I gain as much, if not more that the receiver, the student, or the client. Together were understood each other and were able to achieve more together than any of us could have alone.

I was fortunate to have worked with leaders dedicated to making a difference. They wanted to see the light at the end of the tunnel. These leaders wanted their people to succeed, because they knew that if the members achieved, so would the organization. Certainly there were managers that just "didn't get it." Fortunately they were in the minority. They underestimated their potential at success by falling just short of effort and dedication.

We are all faced with ensuring our teams work. In all cases these Ten Demandments worked. In writing this book, I wanted to share the elements that were consistent across the board. Each of the ten constituted a value and belief that would drive the behavior. I believe that reflective time with this book will help current and future leaders establish a foundation for moving team members to exceptional outcomes.

In the first chapter I focused on the different types of team structures because leaders often apply the same treatment to all teams. In a later chapter you will read about how people are viewed in their teams and the importance of their diversity and the value they bring to the table. This can only be done with the trust and support of the team members, of each other and especially of the leader. Trust, as discussed in another chapter requires that the leader be predicable and provide some benefit to the receiver, namely the team members.

How often have we applied the same rewards to the same outcomes to the same people? How about teams? In Demandment Seven, I propose that if we do not reward teams, the team behavior that we expect will extinguish itself over time. As a leader, you will learn how you need to get out of the way and allow team members to own the project from start to finish, rewarding accordingly. How will you ensure that these new constructs have staying power? Simply by rewarding teams first and stars second.

How do we get to that point? Another chapter discusses how to develop and reinforce Group Genius which recognizes and converts obstacles into hidden opportunities. Developing people requires supporting their experiences during problem-solving and solution-giving processes. Their experiences may not always be successful. The reality is that they will fail. These failures are a result of encountering obstacles that they don't have the skills or the resources to overcome. In those experiences lies the foundation of the supportive leadership; helping people by letting go. The issue of focusing on individuals by leaders goes against how leaders have been successful. They focus on what they can do to make themselves successful, as opposed to what they can do to make others be successful. It is a fundamental paradigm shift.

Join me as you keep your eyes and ears open to new approaches or simply validate your current philosophies. There is real value in seeing those philosophies at work in partnership with Dr. Bill's Ten Demandments.

Enjoy the journey...

Dr. Bill Moskal
July, 2010

Introduction

Demandment One: Team Cultures: If You Have Seen One Team, You Have Seen One Team

Demandment One

Team Cultures:
"If You've Seen One Team, You've Seen One Team"

Demandment One
Team Cultures:
If You've Seen One Team, You've Seen One Team

Relationships, like families, are unique. So, too, are teams. What works for one may not necessarily work for another. Leaders who manage these relationships must understand what motivates people and what inspires them to interact accordingly. Using that knowledge, leaders better guide them toward achieving common objectives. That's the key to exceptional teamwork.

Exceptional teams and turfs share three common elements. First, they each have a group of people (more than one) who works together to get a job done. Secondly, their members work to achieve a goal. The third element distinguishes teams from turfs. Teams work cohesively, in effective and efficient ways toward a <u>common</u> goal; turfs, most often do not have a common goal. Theirs is one directed or dictated by a few.

This first Demandment requires that leaders be willing to look beyond a cookie-cutter approach to building effective teams. No single book, model, or structure applies, yet leaders who find one are often disappointed when the mold they cast simply doesn't fit.

Whether a team's objectives are short- or long-term, each team requires different structures which requires members to set different expectations and requires that the leader form those expectations in totally different ways. A cookie-cutter won't work. One must understand the culture; i.e., what's necessary for success and apply an appropriate structure to the objectives.

Contemporary teams have taken a new and different structure in order to accommodate structural change and the way they do business. The newest generation of people within organizations are no longer co-located; instead, they are sometimes dispersed geographically across the planet, with varying cultures. Geographically dispersed teams don't communicate, or problem-solve, or make decisions in the same way. The real challenge to leaders seeking successful outcomes is that geographically dispersed team cultures are driven by individual efforts, expectations, rewards, and recognitions. However, to build a team one must integrate some of the co-located team expectations, behaviors, outcomes, camaraderie, collaboration and communication so it fits within geographically dispersed teams. Geographically dispersed teams are faster and better at achieving time frames and decisions that are required because they do it on their own.

So, the irony is that they're working in teams, but are really acting as individuals in their own little pods which makes a difference – neither good nor bad. What leaders must recognize is that the culture of a geographically dispersed team is driven differently than that of a co-located team.

Understand, as the leader of a team, that teamwork is more difficult to achieve than working with people on a one-on-one basis. If you have six people in a group, you have to meet the needs of the six and each is very diverse in how he/she operates and approaches problem-solving.

Teamwork takes longer; which is why most managers don't want to spend a lot of time doing teamwork. Instead, they just want to get the job done. It takes greater effort to do good teamwork than working with one individual.

TEAMS and TURFS

The other thing we know about teamwork that's not necessarily a positive thing is that sometimes teamwork works so well in an organization that it ends up creating turfs/silos – smokestacks – where there is very little positive cross contamination between work groups because they do not reach out to each other. They are so focused on the internal that once they become good, it's just about them. The just about me then turns into it's just about us. When they become more mature, they begin to realize that they're actually stewards of organizational outcomes and they begin reaching across silos/turfs to other teams where hand-offs become important.

Many team cultures tend to point fingers at others that we're okay but you're not quite okay. Some of that has to do with allegiance versus affiliation. Good teams are allegiant to each other and tend to be affiliated with other teams, so the allegiance is a stronger driving cultural force. On an individual level we tend to be allegiant to our profession but affiliated with the organization; much like a nurse who is allegiant to nursing, but is affiliated with Community Hospital, or an engineer who is allegiant to his or her profession but tends to be affiliated with the manufacturing company.

Teams tend to take on the same kind of descriptor, behavior, or expectations. They become allegiant to their team and therefore the team becomes greater than the good. Eventually good culture in an organization occurs when the teams begin to understand the greater good of the organization and not the team.

Because it's a long road converting people to teamwork, leaders must remember to focus on relationships as well as results. While leaders can be intolerant of teams that take longer to achieve results, and there is no perfect formula, the ideal is 50:50. It takes a lot of trust of self to become a good leader.

Be patient. Oftentimes, team cultures are difficult to penetrate and often fraught with peril! Trust is required, not just requested. Stay focused on common goals. Participate. Don't ignore naysayers. Convert them each in turn. Remember, once you're in, you're in.

Caution! Being so focused on creating the teamwork and exceptional teamwork of your own group and not paying attention to the greater good of the organization could end up creating a group that is not in alignment with the organization. This dysfunction with the large entity can create dissension and play havoc with the strategic direction of the whole.

When members become invested in a team that is where they derive their meaning, much like a family member who derives meaning from the head of the household who, in turn, determines the values, vision, and core expectations of the family. It's a developmental process. Members reinforce the family values by contributing to society and by articulating what their family believes in. Teams do the same.

For most of us, teamwork is a learned behavior. We have a set of established values and beliefs as part of our team culture, so when new members are brought into the team, they need to be instructed on the culture; the ways in which the team does business. Additionally, the inclusion needs of new members must be understood by existing team members.

THE TEAM CULTURE

What other markers define culture? *Meaning*. Team members identify with the culture that has been imbedded in the "way they do business" within their team. They experience pride and a feeling of wholeness. *History*. This defines who they are and is fraught with examples of rituals and standards and policies and structures that enable team members to point to "who we are...how we got here...why we do what we do." *Values*. Values drive behavior. The team's history provides us with what it values and how these values are brought forward as a foundation for its belief system. Members make statements such as "We value hard work...We focus on the customer as number one...We value open and honest feedback." *Heroes and Heroines*. These are the models that members look up to. They are the ones who have stepped forward, taken a risk and established an identity for themselves that now is part of the team. Heroes and heroines become bigger than life. They eventually become enshrined as the Paul Bunyons of the culture; the super heroes of the group. They remember when "Ann" was part of their group and what she did, or when "Jim" extended himself toward a customer – went that extra mile – and they expect that of everyone. They love to tell about so-and-so, what he/she did, when he/she got angry and when he/she was doing exceptional work with customers, etc. *Stories*. Teams carry the oral history that is described by the heroes' and heroines' actions. Their stories are the defining moments that often are embellished with anecdotes, expanded to fit the audience. People remember stories, not graphs. When was the last time you remembered an exceptional Excel spreadsheet or a Power Point that caused you to say, "Boy, that was exciting"? However, if you tell people a story about what went on last week or last month when you were trying to meet budget or exceed targets, suddenly people bring it up and celebrate it. People in teams and organizations want to hear about those defining moments. These learning journeys enable us to attach a moral to the story.

Also, as families do, teams need ownership of rewards and recognition for what they have achieved on their own. They need to spend time thinking about how they want to be recognized for that achievement, just as a family would. Families celebrate over dinner or a day at the beach because that's what they always do. They celebrate. Teams need to celebrate together in their own fashion, too.

Symbols also enhance a team's identity. We have all been part of teams that display t-shirts, mugs or various trinkets, mascots, etc., anything that says "That's who we are...we're the University of Wayne...we're the phlebotomy team in the hospital...or the maintenance team in ABC Corporation." They share this sense of camaraderie and cohesiveness.

The symbols become the team's foundation for recognition as well as by others in the organization. "Did you see them...those people, the ones with the purple mugs in the cafeteria?" At first they all talk about it with some level of jealousy, but eventually they all want to be part of it because in good solid cultures there's a success model that other people want to be part of. People want to be part of success.

How many of you woke up this morning and said, "I'm going to try to find four people that are really miserable and I want to hang out with them? I need to identify like six or seven losers I can hang with." We don't do that. We want to identify with enthusiasm, achievement, and a positive image because we know success begets success.

Demandment One Take-Away:
Team Cultures

"Teams I Have Known and Loved"

Answer the following two questions honestly and candidly. What are the key elements/components that influenced you during your exceptional team experiences? What worked well? What caused these teams to excel and achieve?

- What is it like being part of a great team?

- What distinguishes this team from others that you have known? What are the "uncommon" elements?

Demandment One: Team Cultures: If You Have Seen One Team, You Have Seen One Team

Demandment Two

Freedom Requires Structure

Demandment Two
Freedom Requires Structure

The paradox of structure/freedom: Without structure there is no freedom.
--<u>Beyond Freedom and Dignity</u>, B. F. Skinner, 1971

Leaders sometimes make the mistake of thinking that creating an unstructured environment is empowering. In fact, the opposite is true. Without structure, there is anarchy. Most of us crave some sort of structure and rules of engagement. I do not suggest that you micromanage, but in navigating the team landscape some rules of engagement might be (1) Know your reason for doing something; (2) Know the advantages for your team; (3) Know the advantages for the people with whom you're interacting; and (4) Understand how the team will benefit from this initiative. Keeping these rules in mind during the process will help everyone stay focused.

STRUCTURE LEADS TO FREEDOM

The interesting thing about Skinner's quote is that for the longest time in my personal and professional life until about 15 years ago, I truly believed you needed to break down all structure. When I was a long-haired, banner-carrying Wayne State University graduate student who did not trust anyone over 35, I would never be willing to openly admit that you needed structure. I opposed all structure. Structure was bad. Then, one day before making a presentation, I was literally singing the ABCs in the shower (a calming technique) when I had an "ah-ha" moment. I had just reread a Psyche 101 text from years prior, complete with its dog-eared pages, written by B. F. Skinner, entitled <u>Beyond Freedom and Dignity</u> (1971). He posits that "Without structure there's no freedom," suggesting that if you don't have structure, you have anarchy. People do whatever they want to do and they do it in such a way that it could be dysfunctional or disruptive – work against the good of the whole, etc.

That made a lot of sense to me and altered my thinking. However, we don't want confining structure; structure that's so tight that people can't have freedom within it. We need to provide them with the parameters. We need to give them the charge, the expectations and the outline and the end target. We also need to share the budget and the time frames that will be required to support the successful end result.

If we create a structure, frameworks that they can work within, then we have an opportunity for them to let loose, break through and still feel comfortable that you are giving them direction.

Freedom to choose, to experiment, to break out of the box, carries with it new responsibilities not only to the team but also to the organization and its clients/customers. This newfound ownership may be more than most team members have felt or experienced. Controls, therefore, are needed. Parameters need to be set; not rules or policies, but rather structured guidelines that clearly spell out areas that are within their jurisdiction. Remember when your parents mandated a midnight curfew? As you gained their trust and confidence, the parameters were extended/opened to enable you to stay beyond that deadline. Parameters set guidelines for behavior.

Demandment Two: Freedom Requires Structure

It is okay to say that some decisions are leader decisions. Some belong to teams. Some areas are untouchable, such as hiring and firing or wage and benefits. These are decisions relegated to supervision. Team members can deal with structure as long as the parameters are clear, rationale is given, and the opportunity to revisit the guidelines is part of the plan.

Team members' styles, the way they prefer to do business, varies with each person. It lends itself to building the team's uniqueness. This contributes to its potential for exceptional outcomes. Leaders need to look at team members' styles and structures because people all approach decision-making and problem solving differently. Some collect data while others prefer to move on to tasks immediately. The latter we call "type A" because they simply want to complete the task. Their time frames are shorter. Others want to contemplate what's in front of them. They want to sort it out, look at options and alternatives. Others, even still, would like to get their hands dirty in resources and spend time looking at best practices from other organizations.

This is not too dissimilar from family members. Team building is similar to family therapy, in that, you have to take into account that, as in a family, we sometimes question how children of the same parents could possibly be so uniquely different. One may be introspective, nurturing, and artistic; whereas, the other, hyperactive and demands to be the center of attention.

Teams are like that as well. So, the assessment of styles is important. The assessment of what they have achieved in the past is important. What are their skills? Are they complimentary? Can they support each other? Can you pull people off the bench to help support that last ditch effort to get the "gold ring," whatever it might be?

> ## "IF YOU DON'T CREATE A VISION FOR YOUR TEAM, SOMEONE ELSE WILL"

The team visioning process is important from a thought process standpoint. If you don't create a vision for your team, someone else will. If people don't know what you're about or what your intentions are and what your direction is, they will start formulating that for you. They will say, "Do you know what that organization is like? Do you know what they really do? They say one thing, but what they really do is..." Thus, a rumor clinic emerges that continually expands, creating an image for you. "I know what Ann's team is like because I worked with them."

So, here's an image of Ann's team, Bill's team, Sam's team, etc. People begin creating images unless you create one for them and say, "This is who we are. This is the kind of team we operate; so this is the way you need to understand this, because we're clearly not the team that you think we are in your heads. Here is what we've achieved in the past and this is the kind of team we want to be moving forward. We are team one. We are the best. We are a team that does it right now. We are a team that gets everything accomplished and gives feedback within 24 hours. We're a team that's driven by outcomes. We are a team that collects data and understands how data is important and how we need to benchmark with others."

Create an image for your team. What's on that business card?

What's on the business card shouldn't be "We're the Engineering department in XYZ Corporation." What should be on the card is "We do windows. We help you achieve a clear vision." Perhaps that's a computer company that does software. That card attracts people's attention.

The Best Buy Geek Squad's image of computer geeks dressed in their short ties with white shirts and pencils in their pockets suggests to us how good these people have to be because they are geeks after all. It's a great study in visioning. They created a self-image for the individual as well as for the team. They feel good about being a computer geek and being part of the team.

What are the benefits of structure for your team? On the maintenance side, structure prevents misunderstandings when everyone has a sense of what the vision is and what the action plan is, how people will be prepared and what's going to be recognized and reinforced in moving forward. I employ the 3Ds: Data, Discussion, Decisions.

3 D's: DATA; DISCUSSION; DECISION

A guideline in decision-making as a team is making sure all the data is on the table prior to having any dialogue or discussion. That's step one. People should research it, bring it to the meeting and say, "Here's what we have available based on this topic. I found this on another team. I did some searching about best practices, laid it out there and had people cut and paste it, roll up their sleeves, get dirty in the data and figure out what's really going on."

In a follow-up meeting, have a discussion about the data. That is when people have a chance to incubate what they went through in the research process. Then, they say, "This is my point and this is what I think will work." Remember, too, the difference between dialogue versus discussion. A discussion might include "Here is what the data is telling me...I'm digging my heels in and here is the position I would take based on what's been provided to the group by me or others." Dialogue, on the other hand, is open discussion where no one actually takes a position but rather suspends judgment.

Additionally, as you move into discussion or decision-making, build in someone who has been assigned as a dissenter or contrarian whose primary purpose at the meeting is to take the data and tear it apart, saying that it will absolutely not work, no matter what the decision, and here are the reasons why.

Contrarians actually have an important role in putting everyone else in the position of defending the group's position. Many relish playing that role, but I think it is more important to assign it to one or two persons and not have it arbitrarily become something that surfaces from five or six members of the team.

At the third meeting, generally the shortest meeting of the three, decisions are made. You should not have to go back to the discussion or the data. It's like an inverted triangle in reverse where most of the time is spent on the data or research and half of that at the second meeting on discussion and dialogue. If you have done the first two meetings effectively, the third should run perhaps 15 minutes.

Visions are big, understandable, and achievable. In generating visions, solicit grass roots input. Everyone should have a piece of it. Members don't necessarily create the vision from scratch, but they have input into shaping it and that's an important piece. Team members should easily articulate it, like a book title, and then be able to explain it in a few seconds. People should feel excited about it. Members bring it to life and insert energy into the vision itself.

> **IF YOU DON'T KNOW WHERE YOU ARE GOING, YOU WILL END UP SOMEPLACE ELSE**

A number of years ago in the early 1960s, I noticed an advertisement on the back of a training magazine. The company featured was DDI (Developmental Dimensions International). On the back cover was a gentleman in a crisp maintenance uniform holding a mop and other cleaning tools. When asked, "Sir, what is your job?" his response was "Sir, my job is to put a man on the moon." He was a NASA employee. He knew his role was part of the bigger vision. His job wasn't just to make sure departments were cleaned; his understanding that what he did, the vision of his unit, department or division, was part of and aligned to the greater vision of the organization...to put a man on the moon. His vision was big, understandable, and achievable. He had a piece of the action and we all want to be part of that action. That's a critical piece. That department infused energy and inspired that man to be excited about maintenance because he knew maintenance was about something greater than his assigned tasks.

Demandment Two: Freedom Requires Structure

I have had organizations do offsite renewal events on a yearly basis where people physically sign their vision statement and re-sign it on a yearly basis. One of the things we know about American culture is that we tend to understand commitment as people signing contracts and oftentimes those contracts from our early heritage were a function of people simply shaking hands and saying, "Yes, I am part of the greater good in alignment with the vision of the United States." What we're trying to do with people in organizations is to say the same thing to them; essentially saying that we are aligned with the greater organization but on a department or divisional level and we are still committed to this vision. Does this vision still relate to the organization's vision, i.e., putting a man on the moon?

I'm not looking at a mission statement; I'm looking at a strategic vision statement. A hospital's mission, for example, might be healing, curing, and providing patient services to the community. Their vision could be "We will be the health care provider of choice in our region." It's a strategic vision and not an overarching mission statement. That's key...that people understand their operational and strategic visions as they build their teams.

Someone should periodically take a look at the visioning statement and become keeper of the visioning process. During meetings, they would be doing such things as ensuring the vision statement appears on the agenda at every single meeting which is one of the biggest failings in working with leaders over the years. The vision statement needs to be articulated once again. Leaders need to put it out on a table and ask if it is still on target. If so, then add people to reinforce it. If not, discover what's occurring that is derailing or detouring the vision.

Hospitals will say patient care is number one, but in only one out of ten meetings, will it be on the agenda. Finance is usually the number one agenda item. On occasion, they have argued and laughed at me saying "That's not true; patients are number one." My reply, "So why don't we talk about them first? Why are we talking about finance?" Finance is an outcome of good patient care. The same thing would be true in an auto company. Are we talking about cars and transportation or are we talking about making sure we meet budget? If they talk about meeting budget, they quickly forget about the vision. Indeed, having someone on the team who keeps the vision in the forefront of the action and incorporates this into the agenda is a critical piece.

Group Genius Vision Mapping is a process I learned while working with Indian Health Service. Over the course of the past fifteen years, I have worked with over 14 tribes, and with this came another big "ah-ha."

My dissertation, graduate work, and early organizational development leadership coaching experiences were rooted in understanding and implementing team building processes in organizations in the U.S., some European countries, and Japan. What I brought into these experiences was my learned team building expertise, of course.

When I started working with Indian Health Service, I realized that I didn't appreciate team building as a cultural process. I learned linear, sequential ways to help people in groups learn how to better interact with each other, but it wasn't group building. It's not inherent in our culture even though we say it is. What are inherent are rewards for individual achievement, for long hours of work, and some increased productivity or outcomes.

In working with IHS, I found that teamwork; team collaboration and team maintenance was all part of the native culture. So what's different? If you think visually of a pyramid... that point at the top...that's usually the leader of the team. They wear the stripes; they set the structure and direction; and, they reward people who accomplish the tasks. Parallel to that, the Native American model: a circle with no one person at the top because in a circle, the focus is on the middle.

IN THE MIDDLE IS THE FIRE

Native Americans say "What's in the middle is the fire." What is the fire? The fire is the vision, the direction; what we all need as our focus. Who's in the circle? Everyone: elders, children, members of the business community, members of the spiritual community and medicine men. A number of people all around and part of the circle have equal roles to play on the fire/vision/direction and the center.

So, when you think about team culture and team maintenance, most of what I have said thus far is really about the pyramid. I am also attempting to draw attention to the circle. Should you discard the pyramid? Absolutely not. What you should strive to do is overlay the circle on top of the pyramid because there will be times when both are appropriate. When in a circle, you need to take the stripes off. Bend the stripes in order to celebrate equally as a team and be focused on the vision as a team. In the pyramid configuration you need to have structure, to have a leader giving direction early on, so people know where they are going and what they hope to achieve.

Most linear sequential vision statements developed in strategic visions are put together in a planning process on 8-1/2 x 11, tucked into a three-hole punched binder placed in the top drawer of a desk which is where it stays. In other words, it's big, somewhat understandable, but is it achievable? Sometimes vision statements become so complex that we put it away because we are afraid to go after it. It doesn't look or feel achievable.

VISION MAPPING

The better model is a five-step open and visual model, like the one described with Indian Health Service. This model is referred to as Group Genius Vision Mapping and includes interactive techniques such as flip charts and computer models to stimulate group involvement and creativity in all steps of the process. First, members describe the present situation, the here and now, followed by the desired future, the vision. The next step is identifying the network of those who will help achieve the vision. The fourth step is identifying the obstacles and opportunities, both of which may surface as we move toward the vision. Finally, specific outcomes are targeted for achievement.

Demandment Two: Freedom Requires Structure

Upon completion of the five-step model, there is also a long-term engagement plan. We need to get this rolling; that's part of the visual commitment piece. Why visual? Because it is a "living" document put in a public place where all members can access it, write on it, cross items out, circle comments or affix additional comments, making it a "living" visual document. In order to increase the ownership, we would take photos of all flip charts, make copies and distribute them to each member of the team. It's a powerful process. The vision is accessible; easy to read and understand; simple to execute because each member has a vested interest in its creation. It's an incredible investment in the Group Genius of the team members.

Demandment Two Take-Away
Freedom Requires Structure

	Disagree	Agree
1. Our meetings are effective; they have a focus and reinforcement of our vision (a presence). We are clear about our direction.		
2. Decision making is understood. We know what belongs to the supervisor, what belongs to the team alone, and what is a shared decision between supervisor and team members.		
3. Roles and responsibilities are clear and understood.		
4. We utilize the 3Ds (data, discussion, decision) to facilitate meeting progress.		
5. We evaluate our meeting based on the following: • Team charge (expected outcomes) • Boundaries and parameters (resources, time) • Support from leadership/sponsor		

Demandment Two: Freedom Requires Structure

Demandment Three

Building the A.R.C.

Demandment Three
Building the A.R.C.

"People panic in herds and recover one-by-one"
<u>Memoirs of Extraordinary Popular Delusions and the Madness of Crowds</u>
--Charles McKay, 1841

How do we lead people during transitions? How do we help them exhibit control over their work space, their destiny, their sphere of influence? A leadership skill construct can help structure that process: the A.R.C. model. <u>Awareness</u>: Skill: Identifying the reality of the situation. Inspiring confidence in others. <u>Readiness</u>: Skill: Getting in touch with your feelings about the change. Exhibiting knowledge via a display of your leadership. <u>Commitment</u>: Skill: Target your energy where you can make a difference. Go beyond the fix and create a foundation for "staying power."

We tend to use A.R.C. on a personal level when we are trying to incorporate new behaviors. For example, if I am aware that I need to lose weight because I will feel better and be healthier with fewer complications to my physical systems, that's *Awareness*. *Readiness* occurs when I purchase a book on healthy living, go online to learn about exercise, buy myself the most touted running shoes and tight-fitting spandex pants, and dole out membership dollars at the local YMCA. *Commitment* occurs when I am fully outfitted; I have read all the books and know full well what I should be doing. I start a walking regime. Week three approaches and suddenly I say "my ankle hurts." I injured it. Now I am laid up. Weeks pass and I know I have to begin again with my routine, but it's difficult, like starting all over. People tell me I shouldn't worry. After all, their "...grandfather didn't exercise one lick; he smoked and drank in the early hours and lived to be 97!" Well...I can now remind myself that I, too, have "good genes." Commitment is tough!

Staying committed requires revisiting Awareness and reminding ourselves to re–invigorate, re-teach, re-awaken, and get ready. Finally, holding onto and persevering and moving forward and getting back up after stumbling ensures that we have the necessary staying power.

Leaders benefit in understanding team mentality and the dynamic of "group think" in recognizing obstacles and by inspiring "group genius" in seizing opportunities. Leaders need to promote skill development and membership commitment to the team's strategic vision. But, perhaps, just as significantly, good leaders understand the realm of their control. They think of it as the Fifty Foot Rule, a metaphor shared with me by my mentor who believed that we can only control those decisions that are within our sphere of influence. The space on the far side of fifty feet could be seen as outside the local control level.

Charles McKay relates the story of greed and speculation that wiped out nearly Holland's entire valued tulip crop in the 1600s. People panicked, of course, because tulips were a form of currency. However, over time, the economy recovered because people made deals one-by-one to barter for what they needed and controlled their destiny at the local level, negotiating through the transition. They were <u>aware</u> of the need for change in the way they were going to do business. As a people they <u>readied</u> themselves by asking questions, collecting data, sorting through the dynamics of people interactions. They readied themselves by becoming quick studies in the process of negotiation. The final step was a commitment to a new form of barter driven by the new models of currency and interaction. The commitment was sustained by the support of the people during the change process. They were able to survive because they were committed to the new change model of barter and interaction.

AWARENESS

Envision the last all-hands meeting you attended where employees were notified of change. There were likely nervous glances or subtle whispers, but the real dialogue began when the meeting disbursed and employees gathered over lunch, happy hour, or in a colleague's office to discuss every possible scenario, real or otherwise, that this change could incite. They rally together in "pity-city" declaring they will never change.

People's reactions stem from emotional uncertainty and the cognitive need for information. Any disruption in team procedures will be met with panic and they will panic collectively; especially teams that have achieved a high level of synergy. In time the outcome of panic will be seen in visible displays such as communication flow problems, in productivity decreases, and power struggles. As team members begin to bump-into-each-other, they fall-over-each-other trying to make sense of transition.

What the end result will be after the change is the last area explored. People are not interested in what the new structure or procedure will look like as that is the least of their concerns. Allegiance is to self during change; not to the team or organization.

READINESS

As recovery begins to surface, individual reactions are also predictable. Members display a level of uncertainty as they try to understand the "announcement." Their first reaction is self-preservation. "Can I recover? Will I be okay? Can I survive? What will I do?"

Understand that panic can be minimized and recovery maximized by providing members with realistic assurances. Answer as best you can, as their leader, why the change will occur, who will be impacted, and how the change process will be implemented. Leaders know that change itself is outside the sphere of influence, but the transition, the emotional/internal piece, can do you in. So, take control. Show your awareness of the "pain" they feel (even though it is a different kind of pain at the supervisory level) and that you see how it affects their professional and personal lives. Listen. Listen more. Instill confidence so that members know they can look to you and feel confident that you will help them. If not you, they will go elsewhere; perhaps another team member or a leader outside the team. Union organizers understand about insensitive or unaware leadership and have some of their greatest successes during times of change. They become the surrogate who inspires confidence.

Additionally, your ongoing role includes demonstrating that you have the skills required to move them forward. These are those skills you are already an expert in. This might include "teaching" skill development in short training sessions built into team meetings. Do some "winning" and watch people begin to rally around. Target your energy where you can make a difference. Help people recover!

COMMITMENT

A successful leader steps up as a steward of change to inspire the team to possibilities, and possibilities begin at the local level. If even one or two members step up with ideas ("Wouldn't it be interesting if ...?"), others may be inspired to new avenues. Leaders making announcements during change need to talk to the team, not to themselves. Because change is a constant, announcements should be acknowledged as a journey, not an end result. In the role of mentor, a leader helps his/her team better understand what the new direction looks like.

I mentioned "group think." Consider its danger. A very few people who feel strongly about change can quickly gather up others to follow without question even though it may not be in their best interest.

The Challenger disaster on January 28, 1986, with its horrendous loss of life provides one classic example of group think. Consider the thousands of minute details that must be in place leading up to launch and the years of preparation. It's mind-boggling. Consider, too, the role that weather plays. One engineer did.

This engineer had done extensive research and was convinced that the O-rings, which ultimately were linked to launch failure, could not tolerate a launch with weather being what it was at that time in Florida. In conference calls with colleagues, he kept bringing up the data. They

Demandment Three: Building the A.R.C.

dismissed his information. He said that to launch would be going against goodness, and in space engineering terminology that meant there was a potential for disaster.

His supervisors did not support him even though they, too, were questioning the launch. Others who questioned never raised their hand to go against the authorities making the final decision. Just prior to launch, someone from NASA asked others on geographically dispersed teams, who had no eye contact, if anyone supported this single contrarian position. No one was willing to be a spoken supporter. Out of 30, one individual became the only dissenter to put his research on the line and say, "We shouldn't launch at this time." He said that "It was against goodness!" We know they did and tragedy ensued.

When people don't have the opportunity to question authority or methodology, or the confidence that they will be heard, or when they are pressured by unrealistic time frames, "goodness" may suffer in ways that seem unimaginable. So, seize opportunities where people actually listen to one another. Stay alert to positive signs of "group genius" where members are free to brainstorm and dialogue about direction and how-to's, possibly even identifying opportunities for change, and where they seriously begin to listen to the contrarians.

Commitment to the end point will require a level of staying power from the leaders and each member of the team. Overcoming the obstacles collectively will support the drive towards achievement. There will be times early in the change that members and the leader will want to "give-up." It is at that juncture that the commitment to the outcome will need to be supported by the leader with resources, time and energy.

Demandment Three Take-Away
Building the A.R.C.

Awareness:
- What parts of the change are within my control?

- What is something good that I can imagine resulting from the change?

Readiness:
- What are some of the actions that I would like to continue doing? (They appear to be working well.)

- What parts are beyond my control that I should let go? *(Actions that are of little value or that are not giving me satisfaction.)*

- If I see a multitude of actions, I must put them in a matrix. In order to move forward, which one can I pull out and put into a high impact area? *(Start with high impact first.)*

- Do I know of others that have attempted similar changes? If so, what are they doing to move forward?

Commitment:
- How will I sustain my efforts? What will give me "staying power?"

- What actions will give me the biggest return on my efforts?

Demandment Three: Building the A.R.C.

Demandment Four: No Obstacles; Only Opportunities

Demandment Four

No Obstacles; Only Opportunities

Demandment Four
No Obstacles; Only Opportunities

"When there was once only one way to go, now there are many. There are no obstacles, only new opportunities."
--unknown author

If we can adjust our attitude to view obstacles as opportunities, we create a positive climate where employees see a path forward as opposed to a constant battleground for mind-share and resources. In the coaching business we call these "coachable" moments – those pinnacle moments when we are faced with challenges and the outcome can be either very positive or very negative, depending on how we choose to handle the situation. Make a commitment to lead by example and maintain a positive and encouraging attitude in the face of difficult situations and you will find that your team will follow suit.

PERCEPTION IS EVERYTHING

Isn't this really about perception? After all, perception is reality. A mix of lines and circles and various depths of color on a canvas some view as Art whereas others aren't quite so sure. Everything we see or experience is unique because we perceive it that way.

This applies to team leaders who, during change or transition, have the difficult job of managing individual "realities." For those team members who perceive only obstacles, the leader's role is to change those perceptions, make them temporary and, instead, open opportunities by

Demandment Four: No Obstacles; Only Opportunities

tapping into the creative solution-giving potential of team members to test their skills and experiences. Leaders have the responsibility to excite members to look to new routes that ultimately lead to new outcomes.

> ### *CREATIVITY ISN'T OPTIONAL…IT'S A SURVIVAL SKILL*

Because "realities" have become internalized, they are difficult to change. They require a new set of experiences, a paradigm shift in feelings. A leader's job is to scale the obstacles down with bombardments of positive and inspirational moments. Anxiety will likely ensue, but without it, there will be no change – only complacency at best; apathy at worst. Remember *"Creativity isn't optional…it's a survival skill"* [David Thornburg].

Managing change and transitions is Job One for leaders! Leaders must be aware of numerous barriers that may prevent team members from moving forward to achieve their stated targets. I have identified ten. These ten are not the only barriers; however, they are the most common, often surfacing with individuals expressing their frustration. The nature of teamwork and the camaraderie among members leads to one or more members influencing others by the expression of their concerns.

> ### *"ENGAGE"*

1. If members fear loss of control, leaders will need to engage members in planning, decision-making, problem-solving, and

Demandment Four: No Obstacles; Only Opportunities

solution-giving. Engagement necessitates the involvement of members within the sphere of control discussed in a previous section.

"PITY CITY"

2. When members feel uncertain about personal benefit, leaders should inquire about team member feelings regarding the project or change occurring. Give members both individually and collectively an opportunity to wallow in a limited "pity city" for a structured period of time. If within a meeting, allow fifteen minutes in an hour meeting. The balance of the time together would then be focused on what would create benefit. What can be done to get past these feelings?

"NO SURPRISES"

3. People in general, especially in teams and organizations, don't like to be surprised. One team I worked with arrived one morning and to their astonishment they were informed of the downsizing of their department by the local morning newspaper! Always set up touch-base meetings in advance of changes; everyone impacted needs to be informed. Be transparent and engaged.

Demandment Four: No Obstacles; Only Opportunities

"BURY OLD NORMS"

4. People drive the same route to work. They prefer to eat at the same table during their lunch hour with the same people. They rely upon the same source (rumor clinic) for their information. They listen to the same radio stations in spite of the fact that listening to others just may give them a balanced perspective. In general we want to change habits. Leaders can work within these comfortable structures by "gently" moving their team members collectively to a new comfort level of behaviors. Leave some traditions in place. Focus on the team's "best practices" and keep them in place. Ask them "What needs to stay in place because we have evidence that it is working well?" "What can we consider getting rid of because the actions do not have any current value to the team?" I have found that conducting a ritual to formally "bury old norms" can allow for the grieving process and can do so with fun and reverence.

"LOSING FACE"

5. The number one fear of most people is speaking in front of an audience. The reason is clear: We do not want to embarrass ourselves, nor do we want to make statements that might be embarrassing. We may, in some cases, fear "losing face" in front of our peers. Our peers know our strengths and our shortcomings.

Demandment Four: No Obstacles; Only Opportunities

We often go to great lengths to ensure that we look good and perform well in front of our peers. The pressure is always in evidence. Are we in fear of losing face in front of our supervisor/leader? Not often. Our team members know that it is easier to pull the "wool over the eyes" of our leader than it is to do likewise to a peer. Peers know. As leaders we can support our team members by helping them take moderate risks relative to new actions that are required to move themselves and their team forward toward goal attainment. Anytime we learn new skills there will be a period of turmoil that inhibits individual efforts and group progress. Failure to "do it right" the first time is inevitable. Therefore as leaders we can help our team by learning from our failures collectively as a group. Conduct "failure celebrations." Applaud, in a structured format, the failures and successes. Celebrate both with vigor and enthusiasm.

"LEARNING CULTURE"

6. Stemming from the fear of loss of face is the underlining question individuals and teams ask themselves: "Do we have the skills to be effective?" There is comfort in the support that team members can provide each other. This is especially true during times of crises. It is an opportunity to teach each other the skills that we have acquired over our tenure with the organization. It is also a time where we can shine. It is an opportunity to risk, in moderation, by stepping outside the comfort zone. Historically

management pundits have referred to organizational change as an opportunity to build a learning culture. It is a time to share and build upon each other's skill foundation.

"SUPPORT SUBTRACTION"

7. Learning new skills and taking on new and different assignments can create more work. In an environment where team members feel the pressure of additional work being added to their current duties, the selling of learning new skills can be daunting. As leaders, we need to legitimize the steps that are required to move forward. Support legitimate "subtraction." Our organization cultures have been notorious when it comes to "add-ons" and failures at legitimate subtraction. This is an opportunity for leaders to model the prioritization process. There is much redundancy in our routine tasks and in our team meetings. We often meet for the sake of meeting. Eliminate those meetings that serve no purpose. If there is no value-add to the meeting or the task, then subtract.

"RIPPLE EFFECT"

8. Changes can and will disrupt other/current projects. This is an opportunity to explore and support the current legitimate projects and subtract those that are not valuable to the team. By

Demandment Four: No Obstacles; Only Opportunities

prioritizing projects, we find opportunities that may have a ripple effect on other projects and, in turn, have a ripple effect on other teams and the organization as a whole. This will be explored in more detail in a later chapter.

"PAST RESENTMENTS"

9. Resistance to change is embedded in past resentments. Many actions can impact our trust in people and the system. People are promised resources that are never received. Members give their efforts to a new leader in support of his/her programs, only to watch them leave the organization in short notice. Statements have been made about security of jobs and working conditions only to find that the spokesperson didn't have all the facts in place. For well intentioned leaders, these are difficult resentments to correct and overcome. One approach is to focus on the here-and-now and the new "how-to's." Listen to what team members have to say about their lack of trust in leaders and the system. This is an opportunity for members to vent and then learn how to move forward. The first step is to get rid of "old cobwebs."

"TAKE ADVANTAGE OF DIVERSITY"

10. A new reality within teams is the fact that there are new and different co-worker relationships. Teams are continuously going

Demandment Four: No Obstacles; Only Opportunities

through an internal fluid change in membership, being downsized, right sized, upsized, and as one member shared with his leader, they are also being dumb sized. Teams, over the past twenty years have also changed in their composition. More teams are diversified both racially and sexually. This has been a bonanza for team diversity, creativity, flexibility and productivity. *(Author's note: In my experience over the past thirty years, teams with a balance of females and males have been far more productive and achievement driven than their all male counterparts. Some of that is due to the coed group being increasingly more flexible and more willing to take on risks outside the normal box of procedures and policies.)* Extraordinary teams take advantage of the diversity and use it to their advantage. This formula consists of initially and continuously addressing the inclusion needs of new members. It also requires that team members open their conversations to a higher level of dialogue. It is an opportunity for them to express new ideas and approaches without critique and ridicule.

Old Reality Thinking:
"There's no money in the budget"

New Reality Action and Thinking:
"Who will honor me with the funding of this project?"
--Leland Kaiser
Healthcare Futurist

Demandment Four Take Away
No Obstacles, Only Opportunities

Dealing with Barriers and Obstacles

- **Identify the barrier(s) or obstacle(s)**
    - What is specifically occurring that is blocking or hindering our team's performance?

- **Develop questions to ask yourself**
    - What am I doing to contribute to the barrier/obstacle?
    - What other factors are contributing to the barrier/obstacle?

- **Develop questions to ask your team members (Be appropriate and encourage team member involvement in identifying the barriers/obstacles)**
    - What are team members, individually and collectively, doing to contribute to the barrier/obstacle?

- **Identify specific actions to address the obstacle(s) and convert into an opportunity(s) (Recognize that every team member has direct responsibility to help the team overcome barriers to performance)**
    - What can our team and I as the leader do to deal with the barrier/obstacle promptly?

Demandment Four: No Obstacles; Only Opportunities

Demandment Four: No Obstacles; Only Opportunities

Demandment Five

Awareness of Members' Value

Demandment Five
Awareness of Member Value

"The deepest principle in human nature is the craving to be appreciated."
--William James, Father of Psychology

Do you see yourself as others see you? If so, the extent to which you do enhances the probability that you will be able to increase your personal effectiveness as a leader. Further, as your versatility increases, the gap between perceptions and outcomes narrows.

> **TREAT OTHERS AS *THEY* WOULD LIKE TO BE TREATED**

Treating others as you would like to be treated follows the "Golden Rule" principle learned at an early age, but if you are willing to invest even beyond and up-the-ante to Platinum, the rule shifts to treating others as they would like to be treated. That requires an awareness, commitment, and understanding about the goals, both personal and professional, of the team members.

How do team leaders apply this principle? First, take time. Get to know what turns them on. Get to know how they want to be rewarded and recognized. Get to know what they value. Learn their pet peeves and how they approach change in general. Learn about their skills outside their work environment. Some may be Scout leaders, or teach ballet, or volunteer at Big Brothers/Big Sisters, or distribute clothing to the homeless. Each member has something unique to bring to the table. Leaders often fail to tap 99% of that potential by looking only at internal,

Demandment Five: Awareness of Members' Value

professional skills.

In addition to investing time, understand that when we create the structure and say "This is what the structure looks like," that's not unreasonable because we need that framework, but that puts people to work inside *our* box. When we learn about the complimentary styles they bring to the team, that's when they are really working outside our box and, instead, bringing us to the box *they* have comfortably lived in. When placing variant styles into a group, you have a powerful dynamic that taps into the value of the team member's preferred style. Some collect data; others make quick decisions or rally around a vision while yet another focuses on camaraderie.

Here is the reality. Research has indicated that we like ourselves. In fact, I really like myself. I like myself because I like the way I make decisions. I like the way I problem solve. I like the way I action-plan and I like the outcomes I achieve. So, it makes sense that I should hire people like me. The data tells us that those in leadership positions have a tendency to hire themselves, i.e., clones. Therefore, instead of having a diverse group with diverse values, beliefs, orientations, and business styles, we load up with people with similar styles. Decision makers load up with other decision makers who make decision after decision after decision while throwing others under the bus. Analyticals hire their clones who generate a boatload of data, but no one feels engaged enough to create a plan and implement it. Outgoing expressive types raise the level of excitement with their multiple flip charts spread about and lots of celebration about each other's being fabulous, yet still no one implements the plan. Engagers, on the other hand, focus so much on the teamwork that they lose sight of the vision. So, yes, we load up with clones, but it's

Demandment Five: Awareness of Members' Value

not going to work.

What can leaders do to balance team styles to ensure the vision and take into account the value that each team member brings to the table?

Former President John F. Kennedy understood the value of individual contribution when he spoke to a collection of 49 Nobel Laureates on April 29, 1962, saying, "I think this is the most extraordinary collection of talent and human knowledge that has ever been gathered at the White House, with the possible exception of when Thomas Jefferson dined alone." Your team could look like that, too, as long as you remember that as extraordinary as your team is, it is composed of extraordinary <u>individuals</u>.

THE OPPOSITE OF TALKING IS NOT LISTENING; IT'S WAITING TO TALK

Secondly, we apply the Platinum Rule by listening. Mark Horstman of Manager Tools said, "...in America, the opposite of talking is not listening; it's waiting to talk." Most of us think we listen, but we don't. When we don't listen, we are not meeting their needs; we are meeting ours. That ties into the original premise that we need to focus on the Platinum Rule.

A colleague of mine, a physician and supporter of new medicine and new technology, also understands about listening. It is a concern to him that in this 15-minute-rule generation where the practitioner is in and out and moving on, that beyond a certain point in time critical information gets lost. As he states and what I believe to be true, "You can have all the CAT scans and 128 cuts...all that you want...MRIs, etc., but the bottom line is if you listen to the patient long enough he or she will tell you what the problem is. They will tell you eventually what hurts and what caused the problem."

If leaders listen long enough, they will learn what people really value, what motivates them and gets them going. That's how leaders show love. I have to define love. This is not love on an intimate level, but this is professional love that equates to understanding, to being aware of the value other people bring to the table and actually appreciating that to the point where you are committed to helping them help you and help the team. William James, the father of American psychology said, "The deepest principle in human nature is the craving to be appreciated." That truly defines professional love.

> **"SOMEONE SAW ME, SOMEONE TOUCHED ME, SOMEONE FELT ME, AND SOMEONE CARED ENOUGH TO GIVE A DAMN ABOUT ME"**

I am personally motivated by a study of early intervention on children by Skiles and Ames in 1966 in Iowa. An experimental group of 13 children ages 30 months to seven years with IQs of 35 to 89 were transferred from an orphanage to an intense stimulation of a mother-surrogate at an institution for the mentally handicapped. Each child was put in the care of a person with Down Syndrome or other mental incapacity for two years. Those in the experimental group scored an average gain of 28.5% IQ points to as much as 52%. Those that remained in the orphanage actually showed a decrease or regression. When Skiles was asked in 1971 at a convention of psychologists in Paris about what made the difference, or how the IQs of these children could have increased when they were being cared for by someone with Down Syndrome or other developmental disability, his response was a surprise to most as it was not rooted in their empirical research expectations. Quite simply, he cited four independent variables: Someone saw me, Someone touched me, Someone felt me, and Someone cared enough to give a damn about me. Merely communicating with another stimulates development.

Teams are a collection of "exceptional" people, too, with their own unique value to add; some, more exceptional than the exceptional, and they need to be recognized for that. Listen to what they tell you. You may find a member who, by age 40, has traveled to nine countries, been incarcerated in a Turkish jail or worked as a missionary; or built a business and sold it for half a billion in order to go to art school. This collection of rich experiences ensures that when these members look at an issue in the team, the horizon of possibilities expands exponentially to become a dynamic environment of extraordinary people breaking out of their shells.

Demandment Five Take Away
Awareness of Members' Value

1. What do you value so much that you would choose to do it whether or not you were rewarded or paid for it?

2. What is the one thing that you are most proud of? Is there something that you have accomplished that stands in the forefront?

3. In what ways have you contributed to your community?

4. What is your greatest strength, i.e., what are you best at?

5. What do you value most in a leader? Is there a leader that you would model your life after (political, religious, community, teacher, etc.)?

Demandment Five: Awareness of Members' Value

Demandment Five: Awareness of Members' Value

Demandment Six

Ripple Effect: Reaction Outcomes

Demandment Six
Ripple Effect: Reaction Outcomes

"When you jerk the socks on the clothesline, the underwear jumps."
--unknown author

When making system changes in any organization, never assume that change will exist without affecting others. It will! When a rock is tossed into water, its ripple effect expands until it gradually reaches the shoreline. The rock has changed the shoreline forever. Leaders, similarly, must understand that their actions directly impact others; however, this should not prevent them from taking action. Remember the importance of pre-assessing high-impact action steps prior to execution. Consider consequences, be accountable, and be clear when communicating change.

As a child, I remember seeing my mother hang our clothes between two poles in our yard, and I remember jumping as high as possible to see if I could help her bring them down. If I grabbed hold of a sock, I set off a chain reaction of clothes spinning around the line. If something dropped, I quickly shook it off, laid it in her basket and off I went. That's not too dissimilar to what occurs in organizations. Sometimes we make a change or we make a mistake. In both cases, actions always have reactions or consequences. Processes link together. Change in one area impacts the others and the "socks begin to jerk."

Change can also create the dreaded rumor mill. Several years ago I worked with a school system in the midst of desegregation. People were being shifted from one school to another and rumors were rampant. We worked with administration by setting up an early morning "stop rumor clinic." This meeting resulted in a clarification sheet given to students as they entered the school door which identified for them those things that *did happen* as well as those that *did not*. It worked. What we had done was take control at the top in the principal's office in order to provide reliable information.

TAKE CONTROL OF THE SPINNING UNDERWEAR

So this begs the question: How do we keep the "underwear from spinning out of control"? The answer is to take control of the ripple effect. As an example, leaders in pharmacy know that a change needs to be made that will impact their internal efficiency as a team. Those changes will eventually become new procedures that will impact all other departments they work with; such as, how nurses fill out forms, doctors' orders, or the transport of medications.

CHAIN-LETTERING

Remember chain letters? You add your name to a list and send it along and with this came the promise of great wealth or some other nonsense. Chain lettering, as I apply it here; however, can actually be used in a similar manner to engage soon-to-be-impacted departments in solution-giving. Involving them early during change makes them part of the first wave of ripple effect, making them active rather than passive recipients.

How might this be applied using a pharmacy example? Let's say the goal of the department is to move medications from their shelf to a second location within 30 minutes. If the department is not meeting this objective, the pharmacy leader should bring together the technicians/pharmacists to brainstorm and identify three solution statements. They write those on a flip chart. Then, pharmacy asks the dietary department leader, for example, for their help by brainstorming three additional methods that have to be unique and not duplicate what is currently on the chart that also could solve pharmacy's problem. They are posted to the flip chart. Next, pharmacy might call the lab and ask them to add three additional recommendations with the same conditions. These, too, appear on the flip chart. Count the recommendations. Now you have nine unique suggestions! If you were to repeat this process with a fourth or fifth department, your options continue to increase and your flip chart is full. Your task then is to select the two or three that you want to implement. Park all the other ideas in a safe place for use at a later time. Finally, you absolutely must alert the other departments as to which actions you chose and you MUST thank them. If you don't, you will likely never get cooperation from them in the future. This is an important piece.

Nearly 80% of the time, you will choose the two or three actions from your own list. So, why go through a more complicated process? Because those remaining 20% have the potential to be breakthrough ideas...the "ah-ha's" that could cause an even greater ripple effect. Additionally, by bringing in internal expertise, you have raised awareness within the organization. Other departments are now engaged

Demandment Six: Ripple Effect: Reaction Outcomes

in change and solution-giving and become aware that they, too, may be part of the first wave of ripple effect. They are active rather than passive recipients. It's a win-win.

So, I believe in innovative techniques as well as creative thinking – at new ways of looking at old labels. One creative thought begets another and another which begins to ripple through the team. Members are not stuck with old thinking; instead, they begin to ask many "what if's?"

My own experience with old and new labels was a lesson I learned while working with Indian Health Services in Arizona. I had set up a retreat for a Navajo tribal council, similar to a board of directors. Prior to the retreat, I was doing the proper facilitator thing by documenting everyone's thoughts on the flip chart. The group was a little subdued, but they were offering information. That was good. When I approached the tribal chief, an elder, he began talking about the "White Eagle...the seven generations...and the vision quest." It seemed as if he spoke for a very long time. I wasn't sure where he was headed, but I wrote a few of his thoughts down and said, "That's good."

The next person, however, wouldn't speak, or the next person after that. The room was still. My colleague, a member of IHS, said, "Bill, I think we need to take a break." I said, "What's going on?" He replied, "You cut off an elder." I didn't know what he meant and said, "He was talking about the White Eagle, which wasn't related to what we were doing." My colleague corrected me. "He was talking and getting there, and he's an elder. You just cut off an elder. No one else is going to say a word." We went back into the room and my colleague encouraged participants back into dialogue. That was an awakening for me.

When we went to the off-site retreat, I felt like I now understood about elders and not cutting people off, so I have my flip chart and I am being conscientious about that. I showed them the notes I had written previously and I showed them the outcomes and targets we wanted to hit. I said, "I'm open...as long as it takes...so what do you want to do?"

ADVANCEMENTS vs RETREATS

The elder raised his hand and said, "Dr. Bill, I have a change I want to make." I, of course, replied, "By all means" and was ready to write. He said, "No, no ... let me do it." He came to the front of the room to the flip chart and began to cross things out. I couldn't see what he was doing, but at the top of the chart, I had written Navajo Nation IHS Retreat. He had crossed out the word <u>retreat</u> and instead wrote the word <u>advancement</u>. He recapped his marker pen, waved it in my face and said, "Dr. Bill, you need to know something: Navajo's don't "retreat," we "advance."

The elder had educated me about the importance of labels and thinking more creatively. Since then, I take people on "advancements"; no more "retreats." I learned the value of moving forward as opposed to moving backward. With new mind-sets, people begin to open their horizons to different ways to approach problems or the solutions they want to develop. Re-labeling or rethinking our approach now enables us to expand our creative thinking processes. Creative thinking creates expanded creative thinking. It's contagious!

Demandment Six Take Away
Ripple Effect: Reaction Outcomes

1. In what ways have your decisions as a leader and those of your team impacted other departments/units?

2. How have you communicated your most recent procedural changes to other departments? How have you responded to their concerns?

3. How have you involved other departments/units in the procedural changes that will have an impact on their processes?

Demandment Six: Ripple Effect: Reaction Outcomes

Demandment Seven

Recognize and Reward Teams First, Stars Second

Demandment Seven
Recognize and Reward Teams First, Stars Second

"Recognizing and Rewarding Teams as we are accustomed is easy and predictable and works for short periods. However, those current, comfortable methods don't really work. They have little or no 'staying power.' What used to work in the past may not have the same utility in the future. Pizza parties are passé."
--unknown author

Teams need the assurance that reward and recognition of behavior that leaders would like to see repeated will occur. One, among many, leadership goals should focus on ways to enhance team advancement. Marshall Goldsmith in his highly acclaimed book on Executive Coaching, <u>What Got You Here, Won't Get You There</u>, posits that some of the behaviors by leaders that achieved outcomes in the past may not be sustainable moving forward. The same can be said about team actions. In order to get teams to perform at exceptional levels, leaders will need to determine the best ways to sustain the energy and the behaviors going forward. Teams will produce. The critical question is whether or not they will continue to produce and how to sustain productivity. The answer? Appropriate rewards and reinforcement. It's very difficult to sustain a team effort if we do not acknowledge it, reward it, or recognize it. One of the basic premises of Psyche 101 suggests that if a behavior is not reinforced or recognized, it will extinguish itself over time. Why don't we reward and recognize teams first? Because it is foreign to us; it is more difficult to assess and to measure. It is complicated. When we distribute rewards and recognitions to teams, we

Demandment Seven: Recognize and Reward Teams First, Stars Second

do so with the understanding that all members of the team will receive the reward/compensation or recognition/acclaim for the service or product provided to the customer. However, in our society, individual recognition has always been the method to bestow acclaim, because we make the assumption that individuals need to be rewarded for their efforts. Certainly, there are stars in every organization. There are stars in every team. They certainly need the recognition for their exceptional efforts enabling the organization to excel. However, we need to consider the other members of the group. My position is that leaders need to reward and recognize both the teams and the stars. We need to reward and recognize teams <u>first</u>! That's the more difficult task. Rewarding and recognizing stars...that's easy. Those will most likely take care of themselves.

The first question that many leaders ponder: Is it fair that all members of teams receive the same distribution amount for a targeted outcome that was achieved or exceeded? Is it fair and just from a leader's perspective? Should it be equal? Yes, because the inequities and balance of power and holding people to a standard will be taken care of by the team members themselves. Leaders should not interfere. The team will take care of itself so long as leaders have set the structure, the guidelines, and the expectations. We don't generally do that; we normally recognize individuals and teams as an afterthought. We acknowledge them, but that's about it.

Be aware of the difference between reward and recognition. In most cases, rewards are seen as monetary, as tangible, as something people come to expect as a result of contributing to the advancement of the organization or team effort. A reward is a stimulus administered

Demandment Seven: Recognize and Reward Teams First, Stars Second

following a corrective desired response that increases the probability of that same response. Generally leaders will reward teams or individuals for "what they make," i.e., the product or service delivered to the customer. A recognition is a special notice of attention. In most cases, we will recognize teams and individuals for "how they make it," i.e., their work habits, attitude, interpersonal skills/relationships and commitment to the process and the customer. Recognitions tend to be the *atta-person, atta-boy or atta-girl* – another way of acknowledging without giving a monetary reward. It is critical to note that in most cases monetary rewards are short lived, but recognitions have staying power. Recognitions have the potential to be remembered and cherished. Money buys a new sweater, but it gets lost in a closet pile and boxed away; whereas, recognitions are shared for years to come with colleagues, spouses, children, and grandchildren. If we reward people and teams, they get 15 minutes of glory. If we recognize people and teams, they can scribe a chapter in their personal and team history.

HAND-WRITTEN RECOGNITIONS

A colleague shared an experience she had recently when she attended the funeral of a co-worker's family member. At the visitation, she noticed a unique item displayed alongside pictures and other mementoes of the deceased. Displayed was a hand-written note given to the person by his supervisor during his tenure in the organization – a recognition for a task performed "beyond the call of duty." This piece of the worker's history was a memory cherished by the worker and his

Demandment Seven: Recognize and Reward Teams First, Stars Second

family. The family did not display a copy of a bonus check. Personal acknowledgments and recognitions have real staying power. Write a note. Write a letter. The power of the written word is amazing. Don't email. Most people delight in retrieving a non-business size envelope from the mailbox with their name handwritten on the front. Right? Put your pen to paper!

An expansion of the reward organization-wide is referred to as a gain-share, an acknowledgment of "how they make it better," i.e., increasing profits, reduction of costs, innovations, process improvements, etc.

A fascinating gain-sharing example appeared in the <u>Naples Daily News</u> on February 21, 2009. Leonard Abess, Jr., sold a majority stake in his Miami based City National Bank shares. He distributed $60 million of the proceeds to his tellers, bookkeepers, clerks, and everyone else on the payroll including 72 former employees. The smallest amount distributed was $10,000 with some receiving more than $100,000. When asked why, he said, "I saw that if the president doesn't come to work, it's not a big deal, but if the tellers don't show up, then we have a serious problem." Granted, most leaders do not have the ability to distribute that level of cash to their employees; however, the story does illustrate the importance of each member and each team toward the contribution of the organization's success.

So, how do leaders reward and recognize teams? Let's begin with the premise that all people on the team are willing and able to contribute to its success. Secondly, as members of the team, the participants have been invested in the team's success and therefore need to be invested in the team's reward and recognition events. In Demandment Two, I described structure as a critical part of the process of the team's work and its achievement. If leaders provide their team with structure around goals and expectations and parameters, the same can be applied to the reward and recognition elements of the team's on-going maintenance. Provide team members with workable parameters and they will tap into their creativity to ensure that the distribution will be fair and equitable.

Years ago, I consulted with a healthcare organization on the edge of financial failure. A series of issues caused the organization to find itself in the throngs of chaos and on-going crises. At the time their financials were horrific. They were in the bottom quartile of the fourteen hospitals in the system. Additionally, the employee satisfaction scores were in the bottom quartile. Much needed to happen. If there was any good news, it was the fact that there was only one-way to go...up.

Following a significant change in vision and strategic direction and significant change management training for leaders and team members, the organization began to turn the corner. After five years, the organization turned the financials and the employee satisfaction survey results into positive territory. Financially, the hospital moved from the bottom rung to among the top three in financial performance in their system. Additionally, the employee satisfaction survey results shot up to the 90th percentile! Customer satisfaction levels followed suit.

A number of new and different structures were put into place. These new ways of engaging employees became the foundation for employee involvement relative to the issues and decisions that directly impacted their internal work and their work with other teams. Employees were active participants in EIGs (employee involvement groups) who focused on structured ways to change their work environment into positive outcomes for the team and the organization. The process was controlled in order to ensure that this would not be viewed as a quick fix, but rather a new way of doing business. The control consisted of deliberately phasing in employee involvement and training over the course of four years thus ensuring that a quarter of the work group would be actively engaged each year. Critical to the staying power was the need to ensure that rewards and recognitions were appropriate and reasonable.

Additionally, the challenge focused acclaims on teamwork and not individual efforts. Early in the process the executive team of leaders was uncomfortable with transferring the ownership of rewards to front line workers. In order to establish a working comfort level with both leadership and the front line, a set of expectations and parameters was set in place. After discussions with leadership, it was determined that $5000 would be allocated to a planning group for the purpose of recognizing the work of the various EIGs. At that time, approximately 200 people in 15 teams were to be recognized by the organization and their colleagues. The planning group of employees decided on a celebration. Their recommendation was to organize what was to become the first of many EIG birthdays. The planning team decided that an image and a mascot were in order. Henceforth the process was called EIGGY's birthday celebration, a recognition for the teams that had participated in the training and the problem solving and solution giving process. They also invited family members to attend with the EIG team members as another way to display their contributions and involvement and share their experiences with family members. They even invited the executive leadership and their immediate supervisors.

Demandment Seven: Recognize and Reward Teams First, Stars Second

EIGGY and OFIA

The first birthday for EIGGY was a rousing success. A six-foot tall wooden character was built by the carpentry department and displayed at the event. All EIG members received memorabilia, shirts, mugs, and of course a plaque recognizing their work. There was entertainment and dancing and presentations. Fun for all.

As a footnote, it is significant to mention that the EIGGY birthday celebration became an annual event lasting for nine years, and more importantly the $5000 working budget never changed. The subsequent celebrations were larger as more people got involved in the engagement work. More families were invited, and most importantly, the ideas for the celebration and ways to get discounts increased exponentially over the course of the celebrations.

A few years into the celebration process a relationship was built to recognize individual efforts, once again reinforcing that stars need to be celebrated AFTER the team. The next component was the development of OFIA (opportunity for Involvement by Associates). In year four the annual celebration included EIGGY joined by OFIA. Naturally, a mascot and wooden figure was built to represent OFIA. Let the fun begin.

Numerous other ways recognize teams such as "bragging sessions" and "failure celebrations," which help people, not only to recognize the work they've done, but also help in skill building as learning sessions for other teams. "Bragging sessions" are great ways to recognize a team. In a particular meeting have team members come to the forefront to do a limited Power Point presentation of 5 to 10 minutes. Let them talk about what they're trying to do, what they felt they had accomplished, and how excited they are about the outcome they contributed. Following the presentation and a brief Q and A with other participants, the audience needs to applaud the effort.

FAILURE CELEBRATIONS

As the team matures, the same process can be structured for "failure celebrations." Oddly enough, failures are a better way to skill build than successes; which we know from history about men and women who have started businesses. Edison failed more than a thousand times before coming up with the light bulb. Sometimes success was inadvertently a part of the process and not necessarily something they were trying to achieve in the first place. So, when the team matures, one way to recognize their efforts is to have them do the same thing they do at bragging sessions, but instead to celebrate a failure. Have the team prepare a presentation to the group about what they attempted to do and where they encountered obstacles that prevented them from achieving the outcome they were searching for, and what they would do differently next time. Have participant/audience members applaud the effort during the bragging session as well as applauding the failure sessions in the same way, so there is no difference. You neutralize them both. Both become learning opportunities.

As an additional recognition session referred to as 'mope, cope and grope' sessions, get it out, talk about it, and figure out how to deal with it. Find out what's happening. This is on the order of "Pity City" with the built in component of dialogue which can lead to some resolution.

LATERAL MOVEMENT ON THE BOADWALK

On a more sophisticated scale, historically we think about progress in an organization or advancement for an individual as moving "up the ladder," but the new reality is moving "laterally on the boardwalk." There is little room at the top. Organizations are less likely to be structured as pyramids; therefore, leaders need to address recognition for individuals in new ways. Organizations can be best described as oblong or soft-sided rectangles. Recognizing exceptional efforts by an individual can translate into leadership over a particular "new" project or learning opportunity. We have to get out of our old way of thinking and that old paradigm to move into another one that helps us recognize things differently. The newer generations especially are more concerned with learning opportunities. The world for Gen X and Gen Y changes daily, hourly and in nanoseconds. Their organizational world must adapt to the scope of the new work and help them adopt strategies to both help the organizations first and themselves, second.

Demandment Seven Take Away
Recognize and Reward Teams First, Stars Second

In the matrix below, fill in the blanks. What is currently in place? What do you need to consider? Consider conducting this same exercise with your team members.

	REWARDS	RECOGNITIONS
TEAM	*In Place:*	*In Place:*
TEAM	*Need to Consider:*	*Need to Consider:*
INDIVIDUAL	*In Place:*	*In Place:*
INDIVIDUAL	*Need to Consider:*	*Need to Consider:*

Demandment Seven: Recognize and Reward Teams First, Stars Second

Demandment Eight

Ownership Is Everything

Demandment Eight
Ownership Is Everything

"If you own it, you take care of it."

When people feel a sense of ownership – car, house, or corporate initiative – they tend to take a more personal interest in its well-being. As is often true of any industry, initiatives become so huge, employees feel too far removed to care. A leader must encourage and enable ownership by communicating overarching objectives and why your team's efforts are important to the organization as a whole. This enables team members to align themselves with the higher level goals. Ensuring that employees know they will be recognized for contributing to the organization's overall success is the foundation for commitment. Communicating to employees "what's in it for them" will result in camaraderie that's both inspiring and beneficial.

Buy your 16-year-old a $2,000 car or a $10,000 car and he/she will care for it the same way. I purchased a car for my son, and on "Day 2," he ripped a major crease into the passenger door while pulling out of the garage. He bondoed the car back together and began saving his money for another one – a Mustang. Rather than purchase a souped up 8-cylinder loaded with boom boxes, he settled for a 4-cylinder coupe. I was surprised, but he rationalized that he would save on insurance and gas. Remember...this was *his* investment. He owned it. Whether you own a car or a concept, you will take care of it. You will wash it and change the oil; you will follow through on maintenance. Similarly, teams working on a project will defend their decisions if they believe they have a stake in its outcome. When you own it, you take special care of it.

WASH A RENTAL CAR?

If you have ever rented a car, how many times have you bothered to wash it or change the oil? Unlikely. In fact, we are more likely to leave a supply of empty coffee containers on the floor. Team members don't wash and polish the annual goals and objectives that leaders place in front of them either. They will perform required tasks, but often only to protect themselves from their performance appraisal. You could attempt to change behaviors, but B. F. Skinner in his last writing stated, "Behavior modification works on 20% of the population if you apply treatments four times a week for three years." Leaders don't generally have the time nor energy to modify behavior. Even if they did, most team members would be likely to resist those attempts. Whenever you draw a line in the sand, someone will be resisting on the other side. So, that's not the answer. What does work involves providing team members an opportunity to shape their future and they will. The added benefit: team members will make adjustments and suggestions to ensure success. Remember, if you own it, you care for it.

The leader's responsibility is to let go and stay close. Lead team members; don't manage them. A colleague is fond of saying that as leaders we need to *"work the force, don't force the work!"* In an effort to work the force, clarify the definitions on a regular basis as you encourage them to participate at higher levels. The tools? Empowerment and Engagement.

How do leaders motivate or empower employees? The answer is always "You Don't!" What you can do is create an environment where the employee feels empowered to move, with a sense of ownership, toward the achievement of the goals. The best definition of empowerment comes from Ron Zemke's book Service Excellence. He states, "*Empowerment is the process of releasing the expression of personal power; it is the opposite of enslavement. Because personal power is already present within the individual, empowerment is not a gift one gives to another individual.*" You cannot give employees any power. They have all the power that they need or want. You can, however, remove the obstacles that block their personal power. As a leader you can remove the obstacles and run interference while employees work on the processes that they know and understand and have the power to produce. Release their power.

GIVE IT AWAY, FOLLOW IT, SUPPORT IT

Engagement involves bringing team members into the process. Mike Peterson, the former CEO and President of Mercy Hospital in Springfield, Ohio, said, "*The way to build ownership is to give something away, then you follow it. Let them test the waters and give them guidance during the process and support it with resources.*"

Leaders must engage people by providing opportunities to set direction. Call it goals. Call it objectives. Call it tasks. Team members need to know where they are going together. If they don't…they will end up someplace else! Teams will achieve. Teams will find a direction.

Demandment Eight: Ownership Is Everything

Teams will end up somewhere. The challenge is guiding them in the right direction. Enable them to have the opportunities for input into goals/direction. <u>Give it away</u> and let them own it. Give them the support and guidance they need while they test the waters. <u>Follow it</u> and give them confidence that you will coach them and guide them. <u>Support their actions</u> with acknowledgement and acclaim and give them the resources of time and money as required. Provide them with the resources they need to learn and accomplish team tasks.

DELEGATING or DUMPING?

What do leaders need to give away? The answer is easy: Make a list of the top ten priorities that you, as a leader, need to accomplish in order to be successful. Once the list is written, circle the top three. Those are the items you give away! Your team members know your priorities. If you give away the bottom three, that is understood as "dumping." If you give away the top three, it's viewed as "delegating." Leaders often question whether they can "trust "that their employees are capable and willing. They are, in most cases, willing. They will be capable if you follow it up by coaching and counseling them through the process. Teach them how to accomplish the tasks. Teach them how to overcome barriers. Teach them how to deal with measurements and teach them about time frames and expectations. Support their efforts with time and other resources that they need to achieve the outcomes that both you and they expect. There was a time when leaders in organizations believed in the value that people brought to the table. The statement often heard was, *"employees are the organization's greatest resource."* This is true and well founded. However, in an effort to engage and empower team members for the future our thinking and belief foundation needs to be, *"the organization is the employee's greatest resource."* Team members need to have the confidence that the leaders of the organization will provide them with the resources, i.e., time, money, staffing, equipment, coaching, etc., to get the job done, and they will. You, as their leader, are the team's greatest resource. You are both the coach and the obstacle remover.

DISCOVERY and THE POWER OF GROUP GENIUS

What should leaders expect from team members who are fully engaged? As leaders we can expect team members to open their eyes and ears to new opportunities. They will develop a collaborative energy that is "group genius." It is the power within the team that builds off itself and its members. It is the power of collective genius. It is the sharing and expanding of ideas. The team members begin to accept each other's new and different ways of approaching problems and solution-giving. In the words of Nobel Laureate, Albert Szent-Gyorgyi "Discovery consists of looking at the same thing as everyone else and thinking something different."

LEADERS ASK QUESTIONS...MANAGERS GIVE ANSWERS

Leader behavior changes from giving answers to asking questions. This is the most difficult part of the transition as it is the most difficult behavior to change and sustain. Leaders were hired and/or promoted because they had the answers. Change requires the ability to focus on the long term. The focus has to be on the knowledge and expectation that team members will achieve the expected results and exceed expectations in this newly engaged environment. Shifting from the current environment to one that engages team members is a long term strategy. By long term the expectation is that this "installation" may take from six to eighteen months to be fully understood and accepted by employees.

In order for engagement to be fully integrated into the business culture a series of assumptions needs to be understood. The first is that employees/team members have information that can have a significant impact on performance and quality outcomes. Secondly, when given a choice, people have the motivation to support the organization and the team's success and well-being. Thirdly, we know that the people that perform a particular job have the greatest amount of first hand information concerning the issues they face and the actions that have to be taken to improve the effectiveness and efficiency of their work. Number four, and most important at this point, is the commitment assumption. When people affected by decisions have an opportunity to be part of the input and decision making process, they will exert

Demandment Eight: Ownership Is Everything

maximum commitment to ensure that the decision is the right one and that it works.

An engagement model that encompasses the four assumptions is "shared leadership." In conventional team structures individuals perform specialized tasks. The emphasis is on job descriptions and there is very little relationship between efforts and finished product/service. In shared leadership the team owns the process and members are cross-trained and rotated through tasks. There are clear boundaries of space and task responsibilities. The emphasis is on work descriptions.

SHARED LEADERSHIP

The table at the end of this chapter is an illustration of the shared leadership model in which many of the tasks originally assigned to managers and supervisors are now delegated to the team members. The primary difference is in authority. In a conventional team, supervisors or managers have the authority. They are the bosses.

In a shared leadership model the tasks are organizing and planning for the work, assigning work, and priority setting. Additionally, improving work processes, communicating to other departments, measuring and taking corrective action are part of the shared work descriptions. Also, the most critical responsibility in this model is shared decision-making. The team has to embrace the authority. The supervisor leader remains at a distance, enables the team, and does not control it. The supervisor typically takes on the role of the coach, facilitator, and internal consultant. Customer satisfaction and business

Demandment Eight: Ownership Is Everything

goals are the focus. Information traditionally reserved for management is provided directly to the team. Their authority varies from company to company...from situation to situation...from the level of skill of the team to the maturity of the team. If the team is held accountable for a product or service it must have the authority to do its job. If it doesn't, it cannot be held responsible for the product or service.

DECISION DRIVER: PASSION or SELF-INTEREST?

If team members are to be vested with the authority to conduct business in new ways, they will also need to employ a new decision making model. In actuality the decision model is no different than the structure we currently understand. What is different is the application of the model. Following is a model that enables team members to be fully engaged. The key to success with this approach is open communication which leads to joint understanding between the leader and the team.

1. You, the leader, decide alone. It's your own responsibility. You are the bottom line. No one else needs to provide you with information or input.

2. You seek information, as a leader, and then decide alone. You can seek information from research; you can go to an outside source or even go to a best practice somewhere else in the organization. You collect the information, sort the data, run it up against any current information and then you decide on your own.

Demandment Eight: Ownership Is Everything

3. <u>You consult with the individual team members or other experts and then decide alone.</u> You make it clear to your team members that you want their expertise and that you're going to run some things by them, but may or may not use it. You need communicate to team members that you will make the final decision. You may or may not use their expertise or input.
4. <u>You share the problem with the team members and mutually decide what to do.</u> As a leader you share the problem, assess the situation, gather data together, decide on alternative action, seek input from all members and decide collectively on a team decision.

OPEN CHAIR EXPERTS

In addition to decision-making, team members need to "own their meetings." A number of techniques can be introduced into team meetings. One technique to open discussion and expand group thinking is the "open chair." For example, a team with nine members, including the leader, should always have 10 chairs at the meeting leaving one open chair. The open chair, whether you use it at every meeting or not is to bring in an outside expert. The team may need to hear from the CFO to discuss the budget. Someone from Shipping or from Dietary may be invited because they have information that you need in your team relative to "hand-offs" or interdepartmental communication regarding a change in procedures. Inviting others to sit in the "open chair" because

Demandment Eight: Ownership Is Everything

they have information and/or expertise enables the team members to make an informed decision. Open chairs builds ownership in the organization and team, and yet, enables the team to recognize that they don't have all the answers. Similar to the earlier chain lettering exercise, occasionally teams need others to come in to either listen or provide you with information or expertise you don't have. It builds ownership, not just in your team, but also helps other people in the organization to understand that they, too, can help own not only the problem and solution-giving process but also the team's transformation.

Leaders that empower and engage their members help build ownership and thus enable team members to ensure "vehicle" ownership; that being the team's path to success.

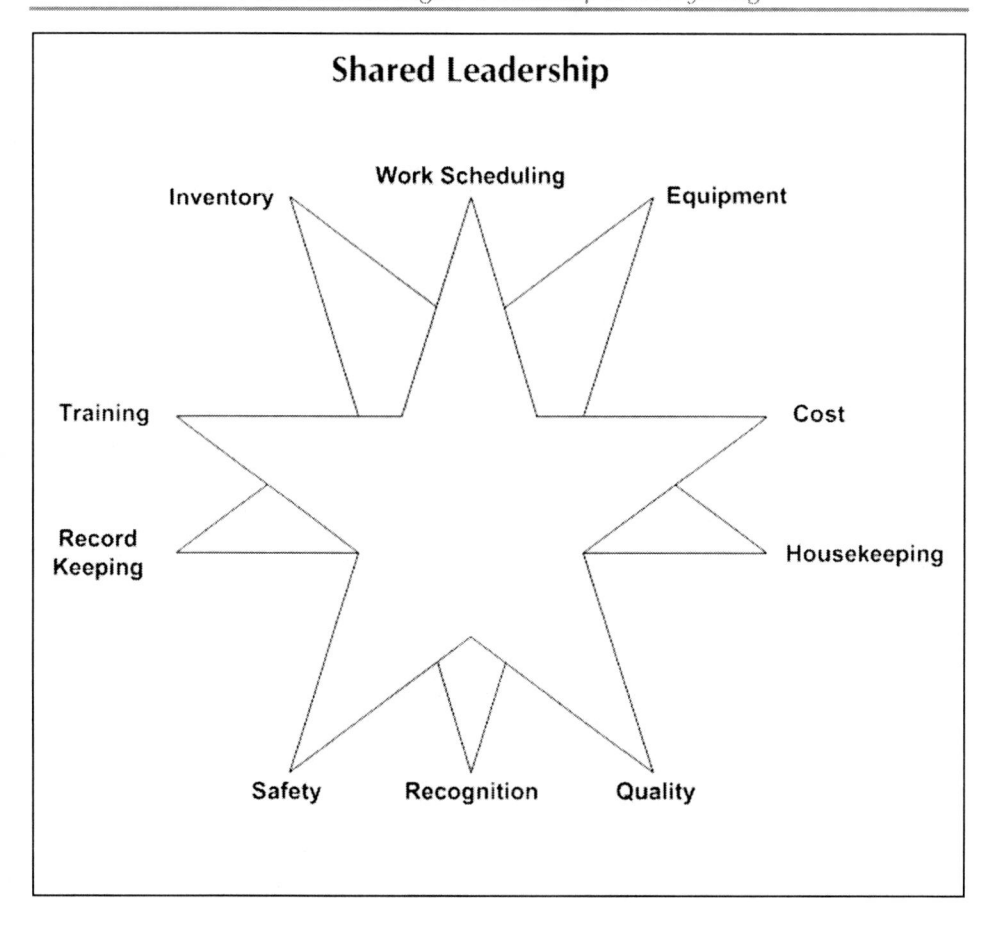

Shared Leadership

- Inventory
- Work Scheduling
- Equipment
- Training
- Cost
- Record Keeping
- Housekeeping
- Safety
- Recognition
- Quality

Demandment Eight Take Away
Ownership is Everything

SHARED LEADERSHIP STRUCTURE

> Identify the administrative and/or operational responsibilities
> that can be shared by team members.

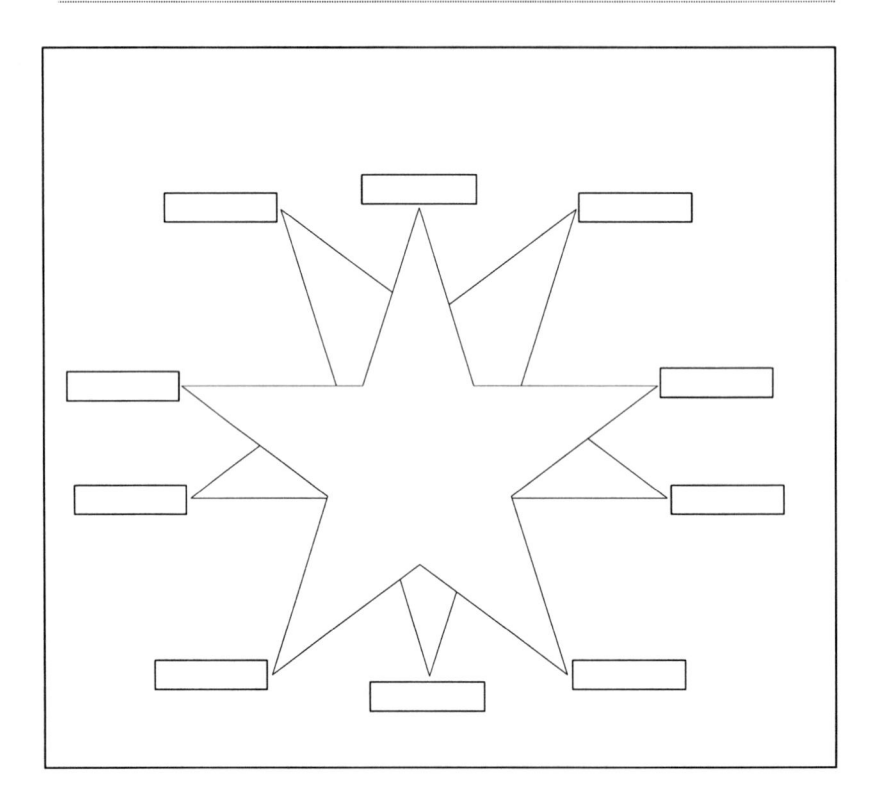

Demandment Eight: Ownership Is Everything

Demandment Eight: Ownership Is Everything

Demandment Nine

Trust, the Leadership Essential

Demandment Nine
Trust, the Leadership Essential
"Trust requires predictability and provision of benefit"

*The infinitive to "trust" requires an **object**. The factors leading to the development of trust may be seen as (a) sufficient predictability of that object and (b) sufficient non-harmfulness or beneficence of the object."*
--Frank Friedlander, 1970

It's rare to find an organization where employees trust management. Unfortunately, in most corporate environments, there is an inherent mistrust for the people in charge. Those organizations that have been successful at building trust have also been successful in achieving outstanding bottom-line results – making trust a critical success factor for any business. To build trust, managers need to promise only what they can deliver and deliver more than they promise – and do it consistently. Clearly define parameters and let employees know what to expect. When goals are achieved, employees need to know how they will benefit. Likewise, we need to be clear about the consequences when the team falls short. Employees will appreciate the candor and you will have begun the process of building trust.

PREDICTABILITY

Friedlander sets the stage: both teams and leaders are objects. The criterion for trust is that people can cope fairly successfully with the object(s). Friedlander posits two major factors leading to the development of trust. The first, sufficient predictability of the object, suggests that people need to feel comfortable that the object's actions will be consistent with past experiences. We "trust" that our car will start every morning...and start every morning. The morning it doesn't; we're disappointed. The second time it refuses to start we have it towed to the dealership; we're disappointed and frustrated. After maintenance at the dealer's, the car may run properly for a period of time until once again...it refuses to start. We're disappointed, frustrated and angry. Trust falls dramatically.

BENEFIT

The second precondition of object trust, <u>sufficient benefit</u>, further suggests that if the car no longer moves us from point A to point B, the benefit is gone. We no longer trust the object to provide us with the expected benefit. The question "Is there benefit for me?" has no answer.

The good news is that most of us are willing to be tolerant of cars, to a degree. We do allow a few mistakes, but not so with leaders and other team members. We only "allow" one leader or team member mistake before trust drops dramatically. Leaders get ONE chance. Make one mistake and it's tough to recover.

We are quick to announce that "others" are not trustworthy, i.e., they are not predictable and do not provide us with a tangible benefit. Leaders are especially vulnerable to trust preconditions. One observed inconsistence and the leader's perceived trust level drops significantly. Not fair? You're right, but that's reality. Unable to answer the question of benefit for a team member and the trust level drops again. Not fair?

You're right, but that's reality, too. People want to know what they will gain. If that's not answered for them, they answer for themselves. No gain equates to no involvement. Why? Because they don't trust that others will support them in the new venture or responsibility. Leaders need to be very conscious of their impact on others in teams. Think "predictable" and act to "provide benefit."

As a leader, you're really a sponsor and a steward to the people in your team. For them to trust you, they have to trust that you'll be consistent. Consistency is the result of follow through; key to this orientation is to focus on people. This is to say that leaders need to be consistent and predictable in their actions to all members of their team. Likewise, team members need to view the leader as fair and balanced with regard to his/her treatment of all team members. This is true both in recognition and for corrective actions. Leaders also need to be empathic and sensitive to the different needs of team members. Additionally, as leaders provide direction for the team, it is critical that the message be reflective of the collective agreement of the team and leader and be consistent in its application.

MENTOR or TORMENTOR?

Leaders should promise only what they can deliver and deliver more than they can promise. One CEO announced to his leadership team of managers and supervisors that there would be "No layoffs under my watch." Needless to say, this newly appointed CEO of six months was trying to please everyone. The fallout from the statement over the next six months was devastating to the organization. Due to major revenue shortfalls, over 10 percent of managers and supervisors and 15 percent of the work force was placed on lay-off status. The follow-up and other subsequent "state of the organization" addresses were viewed skeptically. Few confronted the C.E.O., but most took a passive-aggressive position with regard to changes necessary to sustain the organization. Many leadership team members and employees were reluctant to participate in "change management" activities.

MISSION or MARGIN?

One question I always ask leaders when I coach them is, *"Do you feel like your team members would label you as a mentor to them i.e., a steward or sponsor, or a tormentor, someone who is always an obstacle?"* Sometimes we become the tormentor; preventing people from getting what they need in order to move forward. At times leaders are perceived as the obstacle to achievement of results. For example, the team may be on the right track, they have the resources, the initiative, they're excited and celebrating each other; and then we come up with statements such as "That won't work. We did that in 1948 and it failed," or the classic, "There is no money in the budget." No money is viewed as "favoritism" because some departments receive funds while others are left to fend for themselves with limited resources. Another common inconsistency arises as the leadership of the organization struggles with the "tyranny of the

OR": mission or margin? Which message drives the action? The answer is BOTH: Mission and margin. However, employees often see only the struggle that surfaces between the two as leadership debates and struggles with the horse-trading that occurs on the opposite tracks of the argument. Inconsistency is evident, especially in a service organization such as a hospital that has as its focus the MISSION. Most meetings are consumed with the MARGIN question therefore reinforcing inconsistency in message and actions.

Some leaders perceived as authoritarian are viewed as preferring to control others. This can be evident in large vertical organizations where employees view the leadership as being "rank conscious" and therefore not likely to encourage or engage others in problem solving even though leaders espouse to believe in its benefits. They articulate the value but do not adhere to it as a priority. This can lead to strained relationships between superiors, subordinates and peers. Silos are the results of this inconsistent behavior because leaders act in their own interests and not in the interest of the larger good. Observers often comment that tormentors focus on the "issue of the day." A short term focus works to validate for the leader that he/she is accomplishing objectives in the here-and-now because the longer view does not show results until sometime down the road, often several months later. Those leaders need immediate gratification.

Leaders must understand how to build the mentor relationship with team members. As noted, placing obstacles in front of team members causes them to view leaders in a negative light. Building a mentoring relationship requires not only obstacle removing actions but also consistency in those actions. Trust and verify. Trust your actions and the actions of others and verify for consistency and validity. To move forward invest in front line team members.

TRUST

A model for trust in organizations first developed by author/consultant Jack R. Gibb (<u>Trust: A New View of Personal and Organizational Development</u>, 1978) addresses trust, openness, realization and interdependence. Leaders who work on <u>Trust</u> start with clarifying roles and relationships among themselves and team members. Leaders gain "points" by occasionally getting out of their formal role. Create a circle of dialogue, when appropriate, to openly share ideas, understand individual differences and listen to other points of view. These actions will go far to create an atmosphere of trust and open sharing.

OPENNESS

Leaders working on <u>Openness</u>, involves actively subscribing to a common set of values and norms. The team, as a whole, needs to confirm the ways in which they prefer to do business, i.e., setting norms and guidelines that are supported by the common values. This structure will enable members to better manage communication and resolve conflicts. When teams decide on the norms or expected behaviors for meeting and planning sessions, they are better able to hold each other accountable to those expectations or rules of conduct or engagement. So, openness is a manifestation of trust and therefore becomes that visible sign.

Leaders can often enhance or start building team openness by sharing their own values, a crucial first step in the mentoring process. It models expected openness. Open and candid conversations do not have to be risky. One comfortable and powerful way to open a team to dialogue is to share a story that has had an impact on your life either professionally or personally. Always conclude the story with the moral or the message you want to convey. People like to hear stories. Our journeys capture their attention and imagination. These learning journeys become defining moments that help teams understand "where you are coming from," or what values drive you on a day to day basis, what you believe, how you act, what you feel.

REALIZATION

Leaders working on <u>Realization</u> enable team members to develop ownership of goals and direction. As described in a previous Demandment, engagement of members in the goal setting process gives them ownership. If leaders honestly support team members' involvement in this important process, they will do much to create a foundation of consistency of words and actions that result in increased trust of leadership.

INTERDEPENDENCE

Finally, leaders working on <u>Interdependence</u> beg the question, "who else should be involved?" Given a specific project or team task, members come to realize that they alone are not able to solve a problem or provide a solution without the interface with other members of the internal team or members of other teams. Inclusion of others develops versatility, adaptability, and flexibility. Members learn "overcompensation," that ability of the team members to support other team members. They learn elements of the work/job description that enables them to "step up" as needed. Sometimes that need occurs when a member is absent or is multi-tasking and others need to support the achievement of the outcome.

Demandment Nine Take Away
Trust, the Leadership Essential

REDICTABILITY...In what ways can you ensure sufficient predictability during team building? What can you provide in terms of support, resources, time, etc.?
- --------------

BENEFITS...What benefits will team members derive in the short and long-term?
- --------------

Following are indicators of team success or achievement. These are some of the visible signs that team members are experiencing higher levels of trust. Indicate which of the following have been observed by you or others.

You may also want to ask team members to complete the exercise. In this way you will have a view from the top that can be compared to the collective view from the team.

TRUST HAPPENS...When individuals in the team:

    (1) Feel free to be themselves...always___sometimes___never___
    (2) Feel their contributions are valued...always___sometimes___never___
    (3) Feel listened to...always___sometimes___never___
    (4) Feel a relationship with others...always___sometimes___never___
    (5) Are clear about their roles...always___sometimes___never___

OPENNESS HAPPENS ...When individuals in the team:

    (1) Show interest in what others say...always___sometimes___never___
    (2) Openly express negative and positive feelings...always___sometimes___never___
    (3) Consistent in what they say inside and outside the team...always___sometimes___never___
    (4) Enjoy each other...always___sometimes___never___
    (5) Feel they know other members...always___sometimes___never___

REALIZATION HAPPENS...When individuals in the team:

    (1) Feel responsible to the team...always___sometimes___never___
    (2) Are clear about goals...always___sometimes___never___
    (3) Support the goals of the team...always___sometimes___never___
    (4) Take moderate risks...always___sometimes___never___
    (5) Understand decision-making process...always___sometimes___never___

INDEPENDENCE HAPPENS...When individuals in the team:

    (1) Think about how what they do affects others...always___sometimes___never___
    (2) Feel a strong sense of identity with the team...always___sometimes___never___
    (3) Carry out decisions effectively ...always___sometimes___never___
    (4) Find ways to achieve synergy...always___sometimes___never___
    (5) Collectively keep things "on track"...always___sometimes___never___

Demandment Ten

It's About the People

Demandment Ten
It's About the People

"It's not about Quality or Productivity; it's about the People."
         --Michael J. Peterson

We are our own worst enemies and best advocates when it comes to building relationships in the workplace. Dissension is a man-made problem, but the good news is that we can control how much we'll tolerate and when enough is enough. Leaders need to work to eradicate bottlenecks that slow down productivity and cohesion. Leaders can commit to systematically solve problems and exceed goals by setting aside judgments, fostering camaraderie, communicating expectations, building trust, and inspiring engagement. Ultimately, our job as effective leaders is to remove the obstacles that prevent our people from releasing their power and potential. Most often leaders are the obstacles. Leaders block access to resources, time, schedules, decision-making, and information. Remove the control over the resources, and obstacle barriers come tumbling down.

Delivery of a message that implies that we need to focus our energies on quality improvement and/or productivity enhancement will be received with less than a desirable response. The message is most often translated as, *"We haven't been doing a good job – or a job good enough."* the old reality was wrapped around statements such as..." *You need to do more...You need to work harder...You should do this...You can't do that ...*" Certainly productivity and quality are important. Most people in organizations understand that these are the two most important aspects of their work. However, a constant focus on those elements sends the wrong message. The message needs to focus on people as the resource that will enhance quality and increase productivity. The leadership statements need to read more as…"*You are good…You are capable…You are a special person because of your contributions…You are needed for this project.*" The correct message is that people are our most important, most flexible, and greatest source of creativity, innovation, and strength.

PEOPLE ARE NOT A TITLE, A JOB OR A RANK

Focus energy on people building; building one-on-one relationships. Learn about team member desires, values, dreams and you will learn about how they work and what they value. Find something unique about each team member. Find out what they like to do, what they like to build, the music they listen to and their personal achievements. Tap into their energies and their capabilities. Your team members are competent adults. Treat them as capable and creative and they will reward you with quality and productivity -- both by-products of people working together. Individuals build self-worth by who they are, by what they are capable of contributing, and how they feel about themselves. <u>They are not a title or job or rank!</u>

SELF ESTEEM BEGETS TEAM ESTEEM

Leaders focused on each of their team members will find that individual members will begin to shape their paths and become successful. Success is defined as those outcomes that generate growth for the individual and the team. It's contagious. Other people want to know what the successful person/team has done to deserve the recognition and the success they have achieved. People want to be successful. Success feels good; it feels right. They feel as though they have contributed to the greater good. As individuals experience success and growth, the atmosphere begins to change in a positive way. Others on the team feel genuine camaraderie -- that what is good for members must be good for the team. Self-esteem of individuals begets team esteem. Successful people will begin to seek out others that exude success.

Today, the business culture is described as "the fast eating the slow", which trumps "the big eating the small." There are countless stories of mega-successful ventures like Twitter, Google, Facebook, or Yellowpages.com that may have been birthed in a living room, basement office, or notebook. Similarly, the mom-and-pops of manufacturing and those up and down the line must be prepared for this change in order to survive. Education has seen dramatic change as charter schools proliferate in urban and rural suburban regions. Parents no longer wait for the steam engines of the educational bureaucracies to turn in the direction of the future. Agrarian based schools and industries are forgotten and forlorn.

How should teams respond? They must adjust to these changes by self-correcting, by making changes to procedures before instruction or permission. Teams on a fast track will comfortably challenge decisions and direction. They are not threatened by change; they embrace challenges. Teams on a fast track are turned-on by the opportunity to challenge and overcome obstacles to support higher levels of achievement. There is a significant degree of comfort with conflict as the team matures and builds its esteem.

> ### TEAMWORK IS ABOUT WHAT IS RIGHT, NOT WHO IS RIGHT

Leaders that enjoy collaborative team behaviors are responsible for the atmosphere of camaraderie. These same leaders encourage dissent and value diversity of opinion. In an informal atmosphere team members will encourage each other to pursue higher goals. They understand that the support they receive from their leader enables them to take moderate risks, leading to working toward a common goal that everyone accepts and understands. In fact, where the environment is comfortable and safe and creative and dosed with laughter, team members will attend. The simplest method to measure success is to observe team meetings. Where team esteem is high, members show up to the meetings. They show up early; and when appropriate, they stay late. They want to be there. The driving force in meetings that work well is the mere fact that things get done. The focus is on action steps toward the agreed upon goals. The focus is *not who is right but rather what is right.*

Creativity, innovation, new ideas, new ways of doing business tend to come from the most unusual places; the front line people. Few great ideas have ever been attributed to the leadership of a team or an organization. Leadership's role is to bring to the surface the sources of success, and remove the obstacles. The leader's job is to encourage and enable creative thinking and innovative solution-giving and then "get out

Demandment Ten: It's About the People

of the way." Finally, the leader must focus on making each day for their team members an exceptional day. In this way the investment in the front line is not only about skill development but also people building.

I once facilitated a meeting of small solution-giving groups which was also attended by the top leadership of the organization. Present were five teams that had addressed and solved a problem specific to their department or an issue that was a handoff between two or three departments. Leadership had asked these five teams to present their findings to the executive council. Some members of the council were genuinely interested in the results and had been supportive of the initiative from its commencement. Others were skeptical of the process and the claims of success that were rumored to have been an outcome. One member of the council, in particular, was very suspicious...the chief financial officer. His role and his style gave people pause when he took a position.

At this meeting five presentations were made which impressed all but the CFO. Following each presentation were opportunities for questions from the council to the team members. It was intimidating to say the least. Team members were front-line employees and their direct supervisors. The executive council members were at least four hierarchical levels removed from the front-line -- a very intimidating environment. Generally speaking the teams performed well. A presentation from the dietary department addressed a slowdown in the dishwasher line. They had located the source of the problem and presented solutions that would save the organization more than $200,000 over twelve months. This solution sparked the interest of the CFO. He walked around from the back of the conference table and approached the presenter. The towering CFO, six feet seven inches of intimidation leaned over a petite 25-year-old woman and said, with a smirk, "Why didn't you tell us about this solution earlier? Why did you wait to figure it out in a team process?" He was hoping to display his power and control; however, she looked up at him and calmly said, "Sir, you never asked." Ask questions and you get answers – albeit answers you may not want or expect, but they will be laced with candor and honesty.

An exceptional leader focuses on the people. People produce the productivity numbers and achieve the quality indicators desired by the organization. Team members know their roles and the work that has to be done in order to achieve desired outcomes. When teams work together, they are in sync with each other. Overcompensation is noticeable. That is to say, members know how and when to support other team members that may not be up to speed. Team members also know how to ensure the timing of the project and keep it on track.

A symphony conductor, once during a rehearsal, was keenly aware that something wasn't right. He couldn't hear one particular instrument, among many, because the musician had apparently stopped playing. The conductor immediately called out, "Where is my piccolo?" The conductor knew something was missing. His trained ear didn't hear the piccolo. Exceptional leaders are similar to exceptional conductors; they know when something is missing or out of sync and they step in to correct the problem. They may also step in to call a stop-action until all members are on board, modeling self-correcting behavior.

People compensate or even overcompensate for differences that others perceive as limitations. Several years ago my son's high school soccer team was scheduled to play a non-league game against a crosstown school, a charter school dedicated to educating deaf children. Our soccer team went into the game expecting to run circles around the competition. Our boys made the incorrect assumption that this was going to be an easy victory with minimal effort. Our team's collective perception of the "other guys" was that their physical limitations would impair their ability to keep up with our superior team. Needless to say the outcome was quite different than what our boys expected. Our team was handed a humiliating defeat. Their strategy was not flexible; it could not adjust to the different style they encountered. The boys from the school for the deaf utilized a different set of communication skills to pass the ball, set up the corners, and execute the key game elements. They baffled our boys with their ability to communicate faster and better than our hearing players. The following year the two schools met once again. The second year our team prevailed, but it was a close scoring game. The boys learned to adjust, be flexible, and take nothing for granted. Leaders and teams need to take heed. Not all opponents will play the game as we expect. Not all competitors will follow our rules. Not all adversaries will perform at the level that we think they should in the arena. Exceptional teams learn flexibility and innovation as the key to achievement. Creativity and innovation are survival tools.

ALLEGIANCE vs AFFILIATION

Teams that score high on compatibility and camaraderie are allegiant to the team and its purpose. Allegiance is not an easy characteristic to build. Generally people are allegiant to their profession or their professional association. In hospitals, nurses are allegiant to nursing and nursing practices. They are, in fact, affiliated with the hospital but not necessarily allegiant to it. Nurses are, in fact and in practice, a nurse first and a member of XYZ organization second. This also applies to other groups such as engineers, accountants, lawyers, tool and die makers, computer programmers, etc. The allegiance is first to the profession and secondly to the place of employment.

Is it possible to build allegiance to the team and the organization? Yes. Leaders can encourage and build allegiance by fully engaging the team members beginning with the shaping of the vision, mission, and values of the team. Shaping the vision around the team's collective values will bind the members by ensuring their defense of the team's purpose and direction. The closer we are to our vision, the closer we are to allegiance to the vision and ways to support the team's goals. Affiliation will always be the stronger seed within teams; however, the more leaders can do to enable allegiance, the stronger the glue that binds the members. The focus will be on the people and the people will produce the outcomes.

So, what can leaders do? Conduct people seminars and training. Get them involved in employee involvement groups and Fastrack Teams. Encourage involvement in employee forums. Celebrate successes and failures. Develop identities, where every team is required to develop their own vision, as well as action plans along with goals, objectives, etc. Encourage the development of an image and share that with other teams. Facilitate annual *Advancements* where people have to physically sign on to the bottom line of the vision they have created as a team. Design and develop videos/DVDs of team presentations and achievement and make copies for each member to keep as recognition. Remember to thank all team members. Make time to recognize individuals and teams. Write a "pen and paper" thank you note to show genuine sincerity.

The bottom line is understanding -- understanding each other; knowing that we are different and that being unique is a gift and not a limitation. People that understand who we are, why we do what we do, best serve us. If, as leaders, we focus on growing others, we will grow the team. Team-esteem is the outcome.

> *"If people who do not understand each other*
> *at least understand that they do not understand each other,*
> *then they understand each other better then when*
> *not understanding each other*
> *they do not even understand they do not understand each other."*
>
> *--<u>Appearances and Realities</u>, Gustav Ischheiser*

Demandment Ten Take Away
It's About the People

SIGNS OF SELF-ESTEEM	SIGNS OF TEAM-ESTEEM
1. Yes___No___Job satisfaction is high	1. Yes___No___Collaboration
2. Yes___No___Laughter	2. Yes___No___Valuing diversity
3. Yes___No___Creativity	3. Yes___No___Trust in one another
4. Yes___No___Resilience	4. Yes___No___Loyalty and Shared information
5. Yes___No___High energy	5. Yes___No___Attendance at meetings is high
6. Yes___No___Moderate risk taking	6. Yes___No___Camaraderie
7. Yes___No___Self-correcting	7. Yes___No___Turned-on
8. Yes___No___Members know their individual responsibilities	8. Yes___No___Working towards a common goal that everyone knows, understands and accepts
9. Yes___No___Members readily accept feedback for their individual efforts	9. Yes___No___Work atmosphere is informal and comfortable
10. Yes___No___Communication is open and candid	10. Yes___No___Morale is high
11. Yes___No___Comfort with asking questions and challenging direction and decisions	11. Yes___No___Members take pride in their team's record of achievements
12. Yes___No___Criticism is acceptable	12. Yes___No___They encourage each other to achieve at higher levels
13. Yes___No___Not threatened by change	13. Yes___No___Comfort with conflict